SOUTHERN PACIFIC PASSENGER TRAINS

BRIAN SOLOMON

MBI

Dedication

To Tessa

On the front cover: *Two generations of Southern Pacific passenger steam. On the left is Baldwin-built P-8 Pacific-type 2472, one of 15 locomotives delivered in 1921. On the right is the famous Lima-built GS-4 Daylight 4449, delivered to SP in 1941. When new, both types represented the best of the railroad's fast passenger locomotive, featuring tall driving wheels and high-horsepower output.* Brian Solomon

On the frontispiece: *Distinguishing features of Southern Pacific's famed GS-4 and GS-5 locomotives were the dual headlights in the streamlined smokebox door. The oscillating top headlight was designed to make a sweeping figure-eight pattern to announce the train's approach at night; the bottom headlight is of the conventional variety. SP's other 4-8-4s didn't use this characteristic arrangement; the streamlined GS-2s, GS-3s, and wartime GS-6s featured just a single headlight.* Brian Solomon

On the title page: *The back of this vintage postcard reads "The brightly colored, orange and red, Million Dollar Southern Pacific Daylight speeds daily along the magnificent California coast between San Francisco and Los Angeles—the route of the Missions." Pictured leading the train is GS-2 4412, one of the six original streamlined Daylight locomotives.* Author collection

On the front endpapers: *California sunshine graces the Shasta Daylight at 16th Street Station in Oakland. Lower-quadrant semaphores were still the norm here in 1961, and Train 27 has the signal to depart once the baggage is loaded. Freshly painted Alco PA/PBs will lead today's train to Portland, Oregon.* Bob Morris

On the back endpapers: *Southern Pacific's 1940s-era route map illustrates its "Four Scenic Routes." Typical of railroad maps from the period, this one distorts the United States somewhat to favor SP's service area.* Author collection

Back cover, main: *In April 1991, Southern Pacific 4449 and a re-created Daylight followed much of the route of the old Shasta Daylight on its way to the Sacramento Railfair. Keeping a tight schedule, the train follows the Sacramento River near Dunsmuir, California.* Brian Solomon

Back cover, inset: *In 1951, Southern Pacific used this advertisement for the new streamlined Sunset Limited to stress its enormous postwar investment in new equipment.* Author collection

Editor: Dennis Pernu
Designer: LeAnn Kuhlmann

Printed in China

SP's Sunset Limited *insignia on the side of a corrugated Budd stainless-steel passenger car catches the last light of an autumn day.* Brian Solomon

Contents

Acknowledgments 6

1 The Standard Railroad of
the West and Its Passenger
Service, 1945–1971 By Fred Matthews 8

2 Southern Pacific Daylights 28

3 Four Scenic Routes 82

4 Demise and the Coming
of Amtrak 132

Bibliography 157

Index 159

Acknowledgments

Southern Pacific (SP) has long been one of my favorite railroads. When I was a teenager, my parents, brother, and I took a trip over the SP on Amtrak's Coast Starlight. I still vividly recall winding over Cuesta, hanging from the Dutch door of a Budd-built streamlined passenger car. Although I'm not old enough to have recollections of SP's revenue long-distance passenger trains, I spent many years photographing its freight trains, as well as historic passenger trains. Fellow enthusiasts Brian Jennison and J. D. Schmid further encouraged my interest in SP.

This book would not have been possible without help from many people. I'm indebted to Fred Matthews who enthusiastically supported the project from the beginning, suggested sources for material, lent me his copy of Gregory Lee Thompson's The Passenger Train in the Motor Age: California's Rail and Bus Industries 1910–1941, and composed the detailed personal essay that is Chapter 1. In addition, Fred generously provided many of the photographs featured in the book. Bob Morris of Dunsmuir, California, is an old friend, accomplished photographer, and SP enthusiast. He lent me source materials, provided photographs from his archive, and recalled his experiences with SP passenger trains. He and his wife Rhian also provided accommodations in Dunsmuir. Thanks to John Signor for helping with photo acquisition. Robert A. Buck of Warren, Massachusetts, supplied vintage images and has provided numerous leads and personal connections over the years. Special thanks to the Golden Gate Railroad Museum in San Francisco for providing access to their collection of preserved SP passenger cars. For those interested in seeing examples of the cars featured in this book, a visit to this museum is highly recommended. My father Richard Jay Solomon was very helpful in providing original illustrations, including his own photography of SP trains, as well as giving me insight to period passenger train operations and proofreading texts. John Gruber helped with research and provided personal connections. He and I have traveled in California on several occasions to inspect Southern Pacific railroad stations and lines.

Thanks to J. R. Quinn, Jay Williams, Brian Jennison, and Doug Eisele for access to their photo collections. Special thanks to Michael L. Gardner for use of his darkroom to make black-and-white prints for this project and for use of his photo studio.

There was considerable travel involved with this project. Thanks to Tom Hargadon and to Tessa Bold for providing accommodations along the way. Much of the finished text was composed on hot August days in Tessa's air-conditioned Washington, D.C., apartment. Also, thanks to my brother Seán and my mother Maureen for their support.

Writing the text and selecting images are only part of the process. Thanks to Dennis Pernu and everyone at MBI Publishing Company for their parts in making this book a reality.

Heavily patronized afternoon commute train 138 warrants 11 Harriman coaches hauled by an MT-4 Mountain type. The vantage point from above Tunnel 1 at Potrero Tower was long a favorite among photographers. *Fred Matthews*

The Standard Railroad of the West and Its Passenger Service 1945–1971

By Fred Matthews

Dunsmuir, California, was cold and damp on December 28, 1951. This quintessential railroad town, nestled deep in the Sacramento River Valley, served as a crucial hub for Southern Pacific's operations. On the left, the Portland-bound *Shasta Daylight*, makes its station stop, while on the middle track, steam-powered train No. 328 is destined for Grants Pass, Oregon, via the Siskiyou Line. *Fred Matthews*

My memories of riding, watching, and photographing Southern Pacific (SP) passenger trains may differ from those of most railfans who still recall SP varnish at all. They are likely to remember most vividly the painful days of the 1960s (which in this case began around 1958), when SP, led by the forceful innovator of modern railroading, Donald J. Russell, set out to discourage its passenger business by every imaginable means—negative advertising, side-tracking passenger trains for freight, rebuilding coaches with cramped seating, and in one case even trying to prevent people from boarding a scheduled train.

Until the late 1950s, though, SP was still "Your Friendly SP," a kind of standard railroad of the West—certainly of the Southwest, including California. "Standard" suggests a number of things—including the standardization of locomotives and cars, which SP displayed as its inheritance from a decade of control by E. H. Harriman, the great modernizer of the Western railroads at the beginning of the twentieth century. SP became more independent

9

In mid-1949, Southern Pacific reorganized its passenger schedules. Among the changes, the overnight Oakland–Portland *Beaver* was dropped when the new diesel-powered, streamlined *Shasta Daylight* was introduced. On July 9, 1949, SP GS-6 4463 departs Oakland's 16th Street Station with the very last *Beaver*. The platforms on top of the station once served SP's electric services. *Fred Matthews*

from the other Harriman roads (Union Pacific and Illinois Central) after a federal antitrust suit brought in 1913, but Harriman-trained executives continued in office, and the Harriman style persisted for decades in loco and car design. Southern Pacific equipment was distinctly SP, or "Espee," in appearance—certainly in the 1940s with the standard silver smokebox, but even earlier there was a powerful house style—gleaming, graceful black locomotives, equally shiny Pullman Green coaches, distinctive Victorian depots in Huntington Yellow (a lighter version of Austria's Schoenbrunn Yellow), and twentieth-century city stations, either Mission Revival or a standard Harriman "shoebox" with Renaissance detailing, which came in various sizes. Oakland 16th Street, Sacramento, and San Jose survive (for the moment, in the case of 16th Street) as examples of this style, though with different exterior facings.

SP in the 1940s was a standard railroad in another sense of "standard"—predictability, reliability, tradition, and conservatism. SP passenger trainmen wore high collars and high, stiff hats; they were usually formal and courteous, if sometimes a bit condescending, to passengers. The tone was decidedly Victorian—courteous but also distant and reserved—the polar opposite of the culture of the early twenty-first century. Of course, this Victorian tone came in part from the fact that most SP passenger trainmen of the 1940s had been born before Queen Victoria died in 1901. The Great Depression had meant little new hiring, and older trainmen tended to prefer the regular hours of passenger service. So most passenger trainmen were well over 50, some in their seventies. Mandatory retirement did not apply on railroads.

There was also a "standard," conservative quality to Espee's operating style—cautious, precise, correct. Despite generally excellent track, steam trains were limited to 70 or 75 miles per hour; after the Interstate Commerce Commission (ICC) imposed a 79-mile-per-hour limit for lines without Automatic Train Stop, diesel streamliners observed it carefully. This operating style was in dramatic contrast to the hot-rodding

The popularity of the *Daylight* often resulted in the train running with 20 or more cars. On February 14, 1948, train 98, the *Morning Daylight*, gets assistance from one of the railroad's legendary cab-ahead steam locomotives. No. 4237, pictured here, was a Class AC-10 built by Baldwin in 1942. Southern Pacific had been using cab-ahead locomotives since before World War I to combat smoke problems in long tunnels and snow sheds. *Fred Matthews*

Santa Fe, whose *Golden Gate*s continued to streak down the Central Valley at well over 90 miles per hour, sometimes over 100 miles per hour. SP was smoother and safer, if less exciting, but it was also brisk and efficient. One morning in 1948 my father and I photographed the *Morning Daylight* as it rolled around the curve into Santa Margarita, where it stopped to add a 4-8-8-2 helper on the point. We strolled back to the car and drove through town, only to discover the double-header already blasting off. It couldn't have taken more than 4 minutes.

SP as a "standard" railroad also affirmed another meaning of the term: high standard. Track on mainlines was well maintained and manicured, almost like the British Rail I saw in the 1960s. Locomotives and passenger cars were almost always gleaming and spotless, no matter which of the several paint schemes was present—Pullman Green, "overnight" (and *Overland*) two-tone gray, *Golden State* dusty-tomato red and silver, the handsome Sunset scheme, and, of course, the legendary *Daylight* red-orange-black.

Dining-car meals were also standardized to a very high level, so much so that a recipe book published in the early 1920s sold well and was reissued as late as 1952. Otto Paul Reuss, a German immigrant who was SP's supervising chef from 1922 into the 1950s, compiled it. Aside from checking quality on the line, Reuss also wrote

internal guidebooks for dining-car staff and pioneered partially prepared ingredients like soup stocks, and blends for making biscuits and hotcakes. And SP's entrées, like "Halibut baked in Parchment," "Trout á la President," and "Sweetbreads, Overland," went far beyond the steak-and-potatoes stereotype of railroad meals in the mid-twentieth century. Even hamburgers served in the cost-cutting Hamburger Grill cars that appeared starting in 1954 (as Reuss retired) were excellent and filling.

SP's stations, cars, and locomotives were also standard in the sense of ubiquity—they were everywhere. Certainly on my home turf, the Bay Area, there were far more SP trains than those of its two rivals combined. SP was still the dominant road, if no longer quite the octopus monopoly of the era from 1869 to 1895, when the Santa Fe arrived in the Central Valley. There was a spot in East Oakland, around 5th Avenue, where SP's dominance was expressed visually. SP's five-track Niles Subdivision, the original Central Pacific of 1869, swept through on the flat, while the "new" Western Pacific (built in 1909) had a slightly undulating single track next to it, like an interurban electric line.

Even after branch and some secondary main passenger trains were dropped just before World War II, SP ran a copious passenger service, with the comprehensiveness

This silhouette of action on the Coast Line at Watsonville Junction, California, in 1950 captures the spirit of Southern Pacific's streamlined steam era. On the left, train No. 99, the San Francisco–bound *Daylight*, overtakes late-running local passenger train No. 71, led by GS-5 4459. *Fred Matthews*

Among the finest visions of the SP's early diesel era were its A-B-A sets of Alco PA diesels dressed in the *Daylight* livery and hauling long streamlined passenger trains. With 66 units, SP had the largest roster of these well-proportioned diesels. Here, SP PA 6007 departs the Oakland Pier with the *Shasta Daylight* in 1951. This locomotive is a PA-2, built in 1948 and rated at 2,000 horsepower. *Fred Matthews*

it valued provided in the form by buses connecting to the trains. As Gregory Lee Thompson chronicles in *The Passenger Train in the Motor Age*, the service I saw in the late 1940s was the result of a Depression-era revival. SP had lost much business, and money, to improving highways after the mid-1920s. At the trough of the Depression, SP President Angus McDonald made the risky decision to invest heavily in the passenger business, and not just in the famous streamlined *Daylight* and the premium-fare *City of San Francisco*, but also in a massive rebuilding of older steel coaches into air-conditioned chair cars with reclining seats. McDonald's heir, Armand T. Mercier, continued the renaissance, supporting his dynamic passenger traffic manager, Claude Peterson, in ordering hundreds of new cars in the mid-1940s to re-equip existing trains and inaugurate new ones. Mercier also continued the Depression-era policy of charging very low fares to make the trains competitive with driving. I still recall my shock, upon arriving in Boston in 1959, at realizing that most Eastern fares were too high to afford.

One important element of "standardness" was the unusual continuity of SP's Passenger Traffic Department. Peterson had been the assistant of the influential Felix McGinnis, a San Francisco socialite who advocated passenger service from the 1920s until he died in 1945; Peterson served until 1962. Further, SP had just one advertising manager, Fred Treadway, from 1930 to 1958, who had a large passenger budget until a year before he retired. His "$7.50 to L.A." and "Next Time, Try the Train," billboards rivaled Burma-Shave signs in frequency, and couldn't be missed along the two- and three-lane highways. Overall, from 1930 to 1958, SP spent $30 million on advertising at a time when $1 million was real money.

The Empire in 1947

So, all signals seemed green for a flourishing passenger empire when I became aware of it, around 1947, and began to ride and photograph it. One of my first memories is of the prestigious little *Del Monte*, comprising five cars and a lumpy P-6 Pacific, rapping out its staccato air-horn warnings for the crossings at Burlingame as it worked down to a conditional flag stop. The "flag" was part of SP tradition, a big metal contraption with flag and lantern suspended inside that was dragged from the Mission-style depot out to trackside.

The September 1, 1947, System Form A timetable, of which 115,000 copies were printed, totaled 56 pages and listed about 84 passenger roundtrips systemwide, including 26 Peninsula commutes but not the remaining Northwestern Pacific (NWP) night train or all the Pacific Electric interurbans, which were described only as "frequent service." There was a sizeable intrastate network in Texas, centered on Houston's Grand Central Station. SP subsidiary Texas & New Orleans (T&NO) ran no fewer than 17 roundtrips from or through Grand Central, which, along with the great Victorian barn of Oakland Pier (18 trains), was one of SP's two busiest noncommute stations. Third and Townsend in San Francisco had the most trains, but 26 of its 32 roundtrips were commutes. Houston ran trains in eight directions, including a stub run to Galveston forwarding a standard sleeper from New Orleans. I never saw this remarkable Texas passenger network, which vanished rapidly in the early 1950s. (An interesting point here is how quickly these trains vanished. The powerful Texas Railroad Commission was certainly friendlier to railroads than most other state commissions. Still, T&NO may have had a strong case for termination of its passenger network, since as early as 1938, SP in San Francisco had

Southern Pacific GS-3 4422 departs the Third and Townsend Depot with commute No. 146 on September 14, 1956. This train is scheduled to make the trip from San Francisco to San Jose in 1 hour, 30 minutes. By 1956, most of SP's long-distance passenger trains were diesel-hauled, yet big steam survived in earnest on the Peninsula commute run until the end of the year. By the 1950s, many Lima-built Northerns designed for *Daylight* service had lost their original styling and were dressed in SP's basic black instead of the colorful red, orange, and black. *Fred Matthews*

been very disappointed with the new *Sunbeam* and *Hustler* streamliners, and thought of moving the cars to California.)

My recollections, however, focus on the Pacific Lines, especially in Northern California. That Form A of September 1947 revealed a wonderful variety of comfortable, luxurious, colorful trains that often ran somewhat longer than the consists listed in Equipment Circulars. SP added extra cars up to near the assigned loco's hauling power at schedule speed; the big Overland and Shasta Route limiteds out of Oakland typically had 14 to 17 cars, and I recall a streamlined *Lark* of 19 cars (two for Oakland had been cut at San Jose) and a *Daylight* of about 20 cars passing along 7th Street in San Francisco during the Korean War.

There were still a wide variety of trains. Not only was the *City* now sailing daily, as featured on the 1947 schedule cover, but there were a few branch passenger runs: to Mina, Nevada, though its Tonopah and Goldfield connection had just been abandoned; and Portland to Coos Bay, Oregon, complete with a Standard 12-1-2 Pullman, the last branchline sleeper on the Pacific Lines. A secondary main train, the *Rogue River* from Portland to Ashland, and its overlapping Grant's Pass–Dunsmuir stub, both carried standard sleepers, the latter forwarding its car to the *Klamath* for Oakland Pier. Overall, there were three Portland–Oakland trains traversing the Shasta Route, plus the Portland–Los Angeles *West Coast*, with its open-platform observation, which took the northeast curve at Davis. The combined *Rogue River/Coos Bay* shared the 124 miles of single track from Portland to Eugene. The *Cascade*, *Klamath*, and *West Coast* had through-Seattle sleepers, with the Seattle–Los Angeles trip taking 41 hours. No less

The Oakland-bound *Owl*, train 57, arrives from Los Angeles at Berkeley, California, behind GS-4 4454. Passengers on the platform are probably waiting for outbound trains since the overnight *Owl* is only minutes away from its terminus at the Oakland Pier. In addition to sleeper and coach traffic, this train carried a lot of head-end mail and express business.
Fred Matthews

Steam, smoke, and semaphores dominate this 1949 scene of train 52, the *San Joaquin Daylight,* marching out of Oakland's 16th Street Station. It is destined for Los Angeles via its namesake San Joaquin Valley. Leading is one of SP's massive MT-4 4-8-2 Mountain types, specially painted for *Daylight* service. Behind the locomotive is a heavyweight baggage-railway post office car, also dressed in the *Daylight* livery to blend with the otherwise streamlined train. *Fred Matthews*

than six passenger roundtrips crossed the Sierra (all but the *Overland*) at night.

Three San Joaquin Valley trains (*Daylight, Owl,* and *Tehachapi*) and three Sacramento "locals," plus the Shasta and Overland Route trains, produced real rush hours along the east shore of the San Francisco Bay. In 1948 at Berkeley's handsome little 1913 Mission depot, the heavy tourist/coach *Beaver* for Portland thundered up the hill from Oakland behind a "black" (un-streamlined) 4-8-4 to depart at 5:39 p.m., followed by a heavy P-10 Pacific and the six- or seven-car *El Dorado* to Sacramento at 6:13 p.m. The *Beaver* sometimes ran in two sections, coach and tourist, at peak travel times. The westbound *Overland* was due in at 6:01 p.m., but might well be late, even in those days of punctuality. At 6:20, No. 55, the *Tehachapi,* a long head-end train from Los Angeles via the valley, came rolling in through the factories behind a "skyline-cased" 4-8-2 Mountain. At 6:45 the *City of San Francisco* came up the grade, in 1948 usually behind 1930s-era Winton-engined Electro-

Motive diesels, but soon to be pointed by those Alco PAs that roared and smoked like steam engines. I recall a station announcer later, around 1958, who gave a real auctioneer's spiel in announcing "The Overland *streamliner, CITY OF SAN FRANCISCO*" as the PAs smoked up the waterfront. The heavy standard *Cascade* for Portland, behind another black 4-8-4, was 6 minutes behind (its passengers had come over to the Mole on the same boat). The rest was a bit anticlimactic as inbound trains worked less hard restarting: the *Senator* from Sacramento at 7:03 p.m., the *San Joaquin Daylight* from Los Angeles at 7:35 p.m. A more satisfying sight and sound was the *Owl,* a long train then with seven or eight passenger cars as well as a heavy head end. If only I'd had a tape recorder!

A ferry ride from the cavernous Oakland Mole, plus a 25-minute walk, San Francisco's handsome Mission-style Third and Townsend was largely filled with commute trains, although there were still five daily trains to Los Angeles, plus the *Del Monte* to Monterey and Pacific Grove. Complementing the list of more famous trains including the *Daylight*s, *Lark,* and *Coaster,* was No. 72, the *L.A. Passenger,* actually a long head-end train, due out southbound 5 minutes after the *Morning Daylight.*

The *Oakland Lark,* with its gleaming two-tone gray observation car behind an incongruously ancient 4-6-2 Pacific, was a favorite photo target. The *Lark* was familiar and important in our family, since my father rode it on business about once a month. In fact, he was on the *Lark* that was rammed by another train at Casmalia in 1942. Luckily, he was heading directly to his city office, so was sleeping toward the front of the train

The *Oakland Lark*, with an extra Pullman sleeping car to accommodate high demand during the Korean War, rolls off the Mulford Line at Elmhurst (East Oakland), California, in about 1952. The *Lark* cars were painted in a classic two-tone gray livery. *Fred Matthews*

Budd rail diesel cars (also known as Budd cars or RDCs) were built during the 1950s as a low-cost passenger service solution. Southern Pacific bought just one RDC as a concession to the California Public Utilities Commission, which wanted SP to maintain service on its important Oakland–Sacramento route. Budd RDC No. 10 is seen at the Oakland Pier in April 1957. Despite the state's urging, SP finally dropped its last local service in 1962 when it canceled trains 223/224 the *Senator*. The RDC was reassigned to work the Northwestern Pacific in its last years. *Fred Matthews*

Southern Pacific's *Noon Daylight*, train 97, heads toward San Francisco, railroad direction west of Santa Barbara, California. Lima-built GS-4 4436 has 12 cars in tow, including a heavyweight baggage car. This train was possibly the first victim of postwar cutbacks; it was restored in 1946 but canceled again in 1949 and its equipment largely reassigned to a new overnight coach service named the *Starlight*. Fred Matthews

rather than in the Oakland car ahead of the observation car that was struck and demolished.

We did ride the *Daylight*—No. 99 north— behind steam, in about 1953. Except for views of the lovely GS-4 on the numerous sharp curves, I recall only a full train and the baggage that fell on people's heads when the hogger, in un-Espee style, cracked the whip on one such curve. When photographing commutes on the Peninsula, I loved the northbound *Daylight*, which would come racing smoothly around the curves, marked by a rolling plume of steam, its horn barking a no-nonsense warning. Most vividly, I recall a journey years later, around 1982, when the preserved GS-4 No. 4449 headed an excursion from Sacramento around the Bay and up the Peninsula to San Francisco through *Daylight* country. Thousands of people, including school classes, lined the right-of-way as the colorful vision boomed by, its steamboat whistle sounding the warning. It was like a royal train—perhaps it was. The teachers who took their pupils out had probably been Peninsula kids in the 1950s, and wanted to share this fabled memory.

To complete the mainline picture, in 1947 Los Angeles' glamorous (if inconvenient) new Union Passenger Terminal, soon to star in the movie *Union Station*, hosted six SP departures for the Sunset and Golden State Routes, plus the five Coast Line and four San Joaquin trains. Over the whole 1947 schedule, 27 1/2 roundtrips carried at least one Pullman (the car that went east on Reno local No. 26 returned on the Pacific). Since the longer-distance trains required several sets of equipment (eight on the Sunset in 1940, five or six on Overland trains, and three on the northerly trains until the streamlined *Shasta Daylight* and *Cascade* cut running times), it was a big operation. In 1935, after several layoffs, the Dining Car Department had 2,100 employees, staffing 69 regular assignments plus many extra sections and special runs, which were frequent into the late 1940s. There were four commissaries and an estimated 18.5 million meals were served from 1932 to 1949.

SP's longer-distance trains loaded heavily into the late 1950s when SP intensified its efforts to discourage patronage. Some California Public Utilities Commission

Most SP passenger trains between the Bay Area and Oregon used the tangential and relatively high-speed West Valley Line between Davis and Tehama, California. This shorter route offered fast running and had much less freight than the East Valley Line via Sacramento and Roseville. The Portland-bound (railroad direction east, geographical direction north) and nearly new *Shasta Daylight* zips along in 79-mile-per-hour territory north of Woodland, California. *Fred Matthews*

(PUC) data from 1957 and 1958 (just before they lost final control over service) show not only annual averages, but also operation of extra sections at peak times (which the PUC had demanded). Average daily loading per roundtrip for the year ending February 1958 was 422 for the *Lark*s (240 in the sleepers), 748 for the *Coast Daylight*s, and 246 for the *Del Monte*s. In the Valley, the *Owl*s averaged 353 and the *West Coast* a slender 194, but the combined *San Joaquin/Sacramento Daylight* averaged 629 per day. To the North, the coach-only *Klamath*s averaged only 100, but the *Cascade*s reached 430 and the *Shasta Daylight*s 554. To the East, the *City* averaged 375, the *San Francisco Overland* 323, and the *Mail*s, even with a single rider coach, 110. The *Golden State*s averaged 390 per day, the *Imperial*s (without extra fare) 400, and the *Sunset*s 418. The one clearly weak area was the Sacramento service—the *Senator*s averaged 88 per day, the *El Dorado*s 134, and the nameless afternoon local for which SP was forced to buy a Budd rail diesel car only had 51 passengers per roundtrip.

In allowing the consolidation of the *Lark* and *Starlight* in July 1957, the PUC had tried to ensure that SP would not turn away passengers beyond the trains' normal consists. SP therefore operated 18 second sections of the new *Lark* over the next eight months, including an 11-car first section of sleepers and a 14-car second section, northbound on Thanksgiving Eve 1957. Southbound on Friday, November 8 (probably the eve of a Berkeley–UCLA football game), two sections of 19 cars each were operated, with 27 cars in two sections returning the following Sunday evening. So, through 1958, large numbers of Californians still rode passenger trains, in coaches and Pullman sleepers, when they could.

It's an arbitrary exercise to pick a date when SP passenger service began to decline. Gregory Lee Thompson cites evidence that SP stopped investing in branchline passenger facilities as early as 1917. Certainly most branch passenger services were replaced with Greyhound buses between 1926 and 1938. (SP was part owner of Pacific Greyhound and used the buses to maintain its comprehensive presence in the state.) From 1938, after the state PUC allowed Santa Fe to launch new intrastate rail and bus competition, some secondary mains like the Altamont Pass Route went freight only, and SP warned that lightly patronized trains would not be run at a loss. Indeed, the heavily patronized but unprofitable Interurban Electric system in the East Bay was killed in 1941, with the PUC agreeing that it made heavy deficits. Yet, after 1935, SP invested in new long-distance trains. Train density was thinned somewhat after 1945, but at the time, these seemed like modest consolidations, more than offset by the brilliant new streamliners.

As I recall, we California enthusiasts did not begin to realize that a major decline was looming until fall 1956, when SP applied to cut the *Shasta Daylight* to triweekly

A rainy December 1951 view of Dunsmuir, California, from the rear car of a passenger train shows the passenger station, turntable pit, and an A-B-B-A set of Electro-Motive F units. *Fred Matthews*

except at Christmas and during the summer. At the same time, SP slashed away at the Sacramento service, which had lost more than half its patronage since 1946 as a result of the completion of a parallel multilane highway. Passenger advertising (of the positive sort) virtually ended in 1957.

This watershed moment dovetails with SP records. As Fred Frailey shows in *Twilight of the Great Trains*, there was a crucial exchange in November 1956 between SP President Donald J. Russell (who had succeeded Mercier in 1952) and Passenger Traffic Manager Claude Peterson. Russell made a trip on the *Sunset* and discovered sparse patronage—19 Pullman and 57 coach patrons westbound, 18 plus 93 eastbound. Peterson replied with sharply larger numbers (presumably the totals for the complete trips) and noted that, overall, the *Sunset*s more than covered their direct costs, and indeed, returned handsome profits. Russell, a determined man, was not convinced, and sent a terse reply,

denouncing "information that fools ourselves." Russell seems to have concluded that his passenger executives were either incompetent or misleading him to save the empire to which they had devoted their careers. In retrospect there is some evidence for misleading. Thompson discovered that the Passenger Department's proposal for a streamlined *Cascade* around 1946 had cited the huge success of the streamlined *Lark* after 1941, without acknowledging that more than half of the additional patronage was due to the discontinuance of a second heavyweight train, the Coast Line section of the *Sunset Limited*.

Whether or not Russell ever knew about this, the effort to shrink the passenger service went into overdrive. For a couple of years the PUC delayed Russell's cutbacks, but he was determined and pointed to a sharp decline in patronage beginning about 1950. As SP saw it, by 1956, all but tourist business had vanished from longer-distance day trains like the *Shasta* by 1956. The

In 1950, Southern Pacific still operated *Sun Tan Specials* to Big Trees, California, via a branch from Santa Cruz. This branch was a remnant of the South Pacific Coast Railroad, a narrow gauge line leased by SP in 1887, converted to standard gauge in 1906, and largely abandoned by the 1940s. Big Trees was the location of SPC's disastrous opening celebration in 1880. One of the special trains to the event derailed, killing 14 people. The Santa Cruz, Big Trees & Pacific, a diesel-powered tourist railway, now operates this short section of the SPC. *Fred Matthews*

data give this some support: Coast Line business travelers were shifting to economy airlines (as my father's assistant did after Dad died in 1952), while Shasta Route business travel (competing with much higher-priced airlines) still filled seven or eight sleepers on the *Cascade* into the 1960s. With final control shifting to the federal ICC in 1958 (after heavy railroad lobbying), SP began to see results as numerous trains were slashed from the schedules.

SP's bitter-end tactics alienated far more than railfans and utility commissioners. They seemed to prove the road to be as ruthlessly contemptuous of the public interest as the SP of the 1880s in Frank Norris' *The Octopus*. The ruthlessness may have contributed to the overall decline of operating precision and reliability, which according to Richard Saunders in *Merging Lines* happened on most roads except the Santa Fe, but seems especially marked on an SP whose management may have, after Russell left, lost interest in the railroad.

There is still not full agreement whether SP's passenger operations were a serious drag on profitability in 1956. Most academics, like Saunders and Thompson, tend to support President Russell's conclusions, if not his tactics. But many railfans and rail journalists like Frailey insist that the service was overall profitable. At this point things become technical, entailing the contrast between two sets of data and the question of which set was a better index of "real" profitability. The first set of data, which Frailey accepts as reasonable, was known as "avoidable," "variable," "solely-related," or "out-of-pocket" expenses. "Out-of-pocket" implied the narrowest definition: crew, fuel, maintenance, and perhaps part of station salaries and maintenance. Passenger departments liked this cost standard, but under pressure from above it was expanded after about 1925 to include some share of track and signal costs and most of passenger terminal expenses. The usual term by the 1940s was "variable," including expenses that varied with the quantity (and quality) of service operated, but not including depreciation and other general costs, even though they might fall over time if passenger service decreased.

The opposite method of costing, which SP had helped develop in the 1920s and 1930s, but then shelved because executives feared it might evoke challenges to freight rates, was "fully allocated" costing, whose best-known version was known as "the ICC Formula." This tried to estimate more precisely passenger service's share of everything—depreciation, track maintenance and replacement, signals, stations, etc. It gradually converted senior management. Indeed, SP took the old cost-analysis procedure out of the filing cabinet just about when Russell became SP president.

Fully allocated costing tried to determine the portion of "fixed" costs that were really "variable" over time. Clearly, this included depreciation of equipment, since it had to be replaced, but it also implemented a closer analysis of track,

Last hurrah for *Daylight* 4-8-4s: GS-4 4444 blasts out of Broadway (15.2 miles from San Francisco) to make the 1 1/2-minute run with train 123 to Millbrae, California. Behind the massive Lima locomotive are 13 1910-vintage Harriman commute cars. *Fred Matthews*

The departure of the *San Francisco Overland* brought crowds of friends to the Berkeley, California, station in September 1948, when a cross-country journey was still an event. The connecting ferry left San Francisco at noon, and here train 28's 4-8-4 Northern moves the heavy train out of Berkeley on time at 12:47 p.m. *Fred Matthews*

station, and signal costs to see how much of them could be avoided without or with less passenger service. Thompson stresses that one operating cost that management had assumed was fairly fixed was actually variable. This was the cost, in fuel and track wear, of operating longer, heavier, and faster trains. This (along with lower fares), he says, is why SP's fully allocated passenger deficit actually rose from 1935 to 1941, despite many more riders. The *Daylight* was much heavier than the pioneer Burlington and Union Pacific streamliners, and McDonald's massive modernization of the 1920s steel cars made them even heavier and harder on the track, especially at higher speed. SP's calculation of costs per train-mile rather than ton-mile hid the actual costs from view.

In November 1947, a Cal–Stanford football special rolls down 1st Street at Broadway in Oakland, California. Southern Pacific's mainline shared the street with automobiles for several blocks through Jack London Square in Oakland, an arrangement that survives to this day. Leading the train is 4-6-0 2360, a versatile machine and one of 10 Class T-31s built by Alco Brooks in 1912. *Fred Matthews*

The result of using fully allocated costing was devastating to the pro-passenger case: losses were actually larger than those calculated under the ICC Formula. There was also a snowball effect: as the number of passenger trains on a route dropped, the costs charged to the remaining trains were likely to increase. And new changes initiated by the Russell administration made passenger trains even more unwelcome. Centralized Traffic Control (CTC), which involved remote control of switches and signals and allowed signals to authorize trains to proceed, meant that once-vital stations were no longer involved in train operation, and their costs became solely chargeable to passenger service. On the SP, earlier than on other roads, the transformation of the single-track mainlines, known then as "Russellization"—CTC, fewer but much longer passing sidings, off-track maintenance, and longer and faster freights—increased the cost of passenger trains in terms of more and longer delays to profitable freight traffic. For the 15 1/2-hour *Cascade* and *Shasta Daylight* to make their tight timings on a single-track railroad with fewer sidings meant that high-value freight spent a lot more time on sidings, often on steep grades. From this point of view, passenger trains were not only unprofitable but increasingly threatened the truly lucrative redball freight service.

Frailey defended the use of "solely-related" costing on the ground that SP itself usually didn't apply to discontinue a train until it was unprofitable on a solely related basis. But there is an obvious reason for this. At least through the early 1960s, SP faced thorough and stubborn regulatory commissions. A train-off petition was expensive in legal and fact-gathering costs. So it seems that SP was convinced that losses were large but they still used avoidable-cost data because it would convince critics. The contrast between the two accounting methods also explains Russell's ruthless crusade to drive away passengers. If patronage declined to the point where trains lost money by the narrowest standard, then, and perhaps only then, could they be purged.

Russell's great purge of superb trains left many bitter memories and probably helped in the decline of SP's overall operating quality. Still, it's worth recalling that other roads, even the fiercely pro-passenger Santa Fe, had largely given up the struggle by the late 1960s and earlier on the Valley's *Golden Gate*s. Richard Saunders, in *Merging Line*s, asserts that by 1960 even the passenger-friendly roads had realized that they could never justify new equipment when the 1940s and 1950s cars wore out. Russell was the extra-dynamic leader in what soon became a universal movement.

The only thing that could have saved passenger service was substantial public subsidy. This did come, to a degree, in 1971 with Amtrak. But Amtrak was intended as a kind of "stealth" abandonment, and Russell in the 1950s would never have agreed to something that diluted his control. Nor, probably, would state politicians, who tended to see the SP (in the 1950s) as a bullying nuisance, and (by the late 1960s) as increasingly less relevant. Even today, as California has subsidized three superb corridor services to relieve freeway congestion, these subsidies have many critics who see the trains as wasteful and lobby for rail subsidies to be shifted back to roads. In retrospect, then, the lovely SP trains of the early 1950s were the fortunate result of management's belief in the railroad as public-service corporation rather than as all-out profit maximizers. The fact that some railfans even now cannot accept this conclusion, but believe those wonderful trains must have been profitable, suggests how powerful the profit/loss mentality has become throughout American life.

In this view, taken around 1954, Southern Pacific 2475, the railroad's highest-numbered P-8 Pacific type—a class built by Baldwin in 1921—leads train 224, the eastward *Senator*, toward Martinez, California. By the early 1950s, diesels were holding down many premier passenger assignments, bumping even the newest steam power to secondary runs—a 1920s-era 4-6-2 Pacific working a mainline passenger train was a real rarity. *Fred Matthews*

27

The massive streamlined locomotive with matching red, orange, and black train was among the most memorable railroad experiences. These locomotives, like most of SP's late-era steam-power, were oil-burners. Oil was preferred for fuel because in California, petroleum was relatively plentiful and there was a dearth of locomotive-grade coal along SP's lines. *Brian Solomon*

Southern Pacific *Daylights*

2

Rolling along the California coast, taking in the waves and sun glistening off the water, is one of the great American pleasures. Southern Pacific's Coast Line from San Francisco to Los Angeles is among the most superbly scenic railway lines in the United States. In 1901, following years of construction, the Coast Line finally opened as a through route to Los Angeles. Initially, to reach Los Angeles, trains used a circuitous route via Saugus, but in 1904, SP opened its more direct line over Santa Susana Pass by way of Chatsworth, which nipped 18 miles off the run.

Scenic highlights of the Coast Line include the sinuous crossing of Cuesta Pass between Santa Margarita and San Luis Obispo. Here, William Hood's beautifully constructed alignment negotiates numerous tunnels and tight reverse curves as it descends the Coast Range, culminating with the famous Goldtree horseshoe curve. More famous are the 100-plus miles of ocean-side trackage.

Passengers can gaze out across the vast expanse of the Pacific from the comfort of a passenger train. At times, the railroad line clings to cliff sides, high above the pounding surf; at others, the tracks virtually run along the beach.

The Coast was opened in the era of heavily varnished wooden passenger cars, ornately decorated in the styles of the Victorian and Edwardian periods. During the early twentieth century, under E. H. Harriman, SP began phasing out wooden equipment in favor of new, heavier, and substantially safer all-steel passenger cars.

Through passenger service here began on March 31, 1901. Among the premier passenger trains on the Coast Line in its first couple of decades was the deluxe San Francisco–to–New Orleans *Sunset Limited*, which had been routed via SP's original route to Los Angeles over Tehachapi. Where the *Sunset Limited* variously operated on a weekly or biweekly schedule, Southern Pacific's *Sunset Express* was a daily overnight train, connecting San Francisco, Los Angeles, and New Orleans.

One of the most posh trains on the SP in the first decade of the twentieth century was the *Shore Line Limited*, an exclusively first-class parlor-car train that operated on a 13 1/2-hour schedule between San Francisco and Los Angeles. At the rear of the train was a heavyweight open-end observation car. At a time when only a few privileged people had phones in their homes, SP advertised that the *Shore Line Limited* offered phone connections for 30 minutes prior to departure at both San Francisco and Los Angeles.

The *Coast Line Limited* operated for just two years as the daytime coach train. It was supplanted by the *Coaster* in 1903, a similar day-coach train that operated until 1917, when it was canceled as a result of the traffic demands resulting from World War I. In the mid-1920s, SP revived the *Coaster* as a name train but operated it as an overnight coach and sleeper service. In 1910, SP introduced one its most famous trains, the all-Pullman sleeping-car express *Lark,* operating as trains 75 and 76. In addition to these through services were local passenger trains, most of them nameless, collecting passengers at smaller towns and cities along the route.

SP's 4-6-2 Pacifics were standard locomotives assigned to work the Coast. Since a single Pacific was not capable of maintaining track speed on the ascent of Cuesta, most westward (San Francisco–bound) trains paused at San Luis Obispo for a helper.

In 1902, a year after the Coast Line opened to through traffic, Southern Pacific 4-6-0 2288 rests at Arcade Depot in Los Angeles. This locomotive is brand new and one of 18 Vauclain Compounds built by Baldwin, SP Class T-26. These were relatively fast engines intended for passenger work. Compounds were designed to reuse exhausted steam to improve thermal efficiency. However, high maintenance costs brought on by the more complex equipment tended to outweigh efficiency advantages and many compounds were rebuilt for conventional operation. *F. J. Peterson, author collection*

This pre–World War I period view depicts Southern Pacific's San Francisco–Los Angeles overnight sleeper train, the *Lark*. SP trains of the period maintained a clean, conventional appearance. Locomotive 3028, a 4-4-2 Atlantic built in 1904 and featuring very tall (81-inch diameter) driving wheels, was a fast machine designed to haul SP's premier trains. When SP switched to all-steel passenger cars, the greater weight required more powerful locomotives and the 4-6-2 Pacific was adopted as standard power. *Author collection*

Southern Pacific's famous limiteds garnered most of the glory, but its workhorse local trains served the majority of smaller communities along its lines. Before highways became dominant, the public relied on local trains for transport. SP train 72, the *Los Angeles Passenger*, makes its station stop at San Luis Obispo, California, on July 26, 1937. Leading is P-5 Pacific 2447, a typical pre–World War I passenger locomotive. *Otto Perry, Denver Public Library Western History Collection*

Daylight

By the mid-1920s, increased automobile usage and state-sponsored highways had begun to seriously erode Southern Pacific's local patronage. Its long-distance services were less affected and ridership remained strong. Gregory Lee Thompson notes in *The Passenger Train in the Motor Age* that SP's long-distance trains served affluent urban passengers. On April 28, 1922, SP inaugurated an experimental luxury service called the *Daylight Limited* to cater to the lucrative upscale San Francisco–Los Angeles travel market. Running on an expedited 13-hour schedule, it initially ran only on Fridays and Saturdays until the end of November. A heavy Pacific, five 60-foot Harriman steel coaches, and a dining car comprised the typical consist.

As with many premier trains, service was intended for seasonal travel and resumed operation in April 1923. In its second season, the *Daylight Limited* was gradually expanded so by mid-July it was on a daily schedule. The train's popularity demanded additional capacity, and according to Richard K. Wright in his book *Southern Pacific Daylight*, during 1923 SP assigned to service American Car & Foundry–built 72-foot steel coaches that featured 90 high-back seats per car, 18 more seats than the 60-foot cars. The new cars were equipped with six-wheel trucks that made for a much smoother ride down the coast. While six-axle Pullman sleepers were the norm, coaches using this arrangement were very unusual, and Wright notes that the *Daylight Limited* was among the first SP trains to use such equipment. In addition, the train carried an unusually heavy six-axle open-end observation car. Unlike the more common open-end

Southern Pacific 4449 is the last surviving streamlined *Daylight* steam locomotive. Among the most expensive passenger trains ever built, SP's original *Daylight*s were also some the most successful and best-known trains in the United States. The flashy *Daylight* was a thrill to all who experienced it pass by. *Brian Solomon*

32

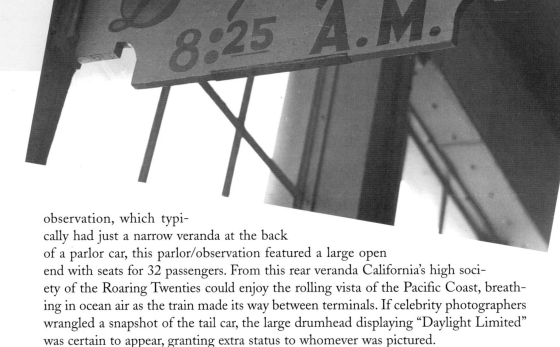

A train indicator at SP's Third and Townsend Depot in San Francisco alerts passengers to the track on which the *Coast Daylight* is boarding. Part of the *Daylight's* aesthetic was this stylized logo featured on the original streamlined trains and company literature.
Bob Morris

observation, which typi-
cally had just a narrow veranda at the back
of a parlor car, this parlor/observation featured a large open
end with seats for 32 passengers. From this rear veranda California's high society of the Roaring Twenties could enjoy the rolling vista of the Pacific Coast, breath-
ing in ocean air as the train made its way between terminals. If celebrity photographers
wrangled a snapshot of the tail car, the large drumhead displaying "Daylight Limited"
was certain to appear, granting extra status to whomever was pictured.

During the 1920s, SP made a number of nominal improvements to the *Daylight
Limited*. By April 1924, SP trimmed its schedule to a 12-hour run. According to
Wright, in 1927 the *Daylight Limited* was the world's longest nonstop run (it only
stopped twice for fuel and water, but not once for passengers). This even beat out nonstop runs claimed by British trains like the legendary *Flying Scotsman*. The primary dif-
ference was that while Britain's express trains didn't run as far, they were equipped with
water scoops to take water from track pans. By this time, the *Daylight Limited* was
billed as "the fastest train in the West," never mind what the *other* railroads might be
doing. More important to *Daylight* passengers than gimmicks was the fact that it was
almost 2 hours faster than other Coast trains.

In 1928, "*Limited*" was dropped from the name and a few intermediate stops were
added back into the schedule. By this time the old wooden parlor/observation cars were
replaced with modern all-steel, 83-foot–6-inch observation cars.

In the 1920s, the cars were cooled using paddle fans, which needed to do their best
on scorching hot summer days. Initially, *Daylight* cars were painted in the same drab
Pullman olive green that adorned most passenger cars across the country. According to
Dennis Ryan and Joseph Shine in *Southern Pacific Passenger Trains, Vol. 2*, SP President

Paul Shoup wanted to make the *Daylight* truly distinctive so as early as 1926, he urged brighter colors for the train to set apart the *Daylight* from other services. Another benefit of the new paint, however, was to reflect the sun and keep the cars cooler. Although initially vetoed by the operating men, in 1929 Shoup prevailed and SP refurbished three sets of equipment painted in a classy "pearl gray" livery with gold lettering. Previously, other railroads had toyed with brightly colored trains, most famously Pennsylvania Railroad's 1898 *Pennsylvania Limited*, known as the "Yellow Kid" for its bright yellow livery, and New York & New England's legendary "White Train." This, however, was SP's first adventure with a specially painted train, and *Sunset Limited's* parlor/observation cars were also treated with light paint. This livery proved too difficult to keep clean, however, and the cars were soon repainted, but the failed experiment foreshadowed the application of an even bolder livery on the *Daylight*.

Heavier cars, high patronage, and exceptional scheduling demands required more power than SP's 4-6-2 Pacifics could deliver, and during the early 1930s, newer, heavier, and more-powerful 4-8-2 Mountain types were assigned to haul the *Daylight*. SP's passenger traffic waned considerably during the 1920s, but *Daylight* and other luxury runs generally faired well. By 1931, tough times had hit *Daylight's* patronage and Southern Pacific's reaction was to scale back operations. SP cut the *Shore Line* and rescheduled the *Daylight* to accommodate additional station stops, while eliminating the luxurious open-ended observation cars.

As the Great Depression worsened, SP's passenger levels and revenues plummeted. Between 1929 and 1933, revenue from intrastate services like the *Daylight* had fallen by 64 percent, and interstate revenues by 68 percent. By the end of 1933, passenger numbers were at their lowest levels in 35 years.

Poor revenues, low ridership, and a gloomy forecast did not prevent SP from improving services where it could. Among SP's significant innovations was its use of air conditioning, beginning in 1932; by 1936, SP was advertising air conditioning on many of its long-distance trains.

SP Ponders Innovation

Angus McDonald assumed the presidency of Southern Pacific in 1933, replacing Paul Shoup. McDonald inspired innovation, creativity, and action among his subordinates. To address the steep declines in its passenger business, Southern Pacific hired for advice the well-known ad agency Lord & Thomas. In the July 1986 issue of *TRAINS Magazine*, Don Hofsommer wrote that traditionally SP had relied on a passive philosophy: operate trains and passengers will ride them. Lord & Thomas urged a proactive approach, specifically suggesting advertising and lowering fares. It also suggested SP develop its San Francisco (Oakland)-to-Sacramento route using high-speed internal combustion railcars. In 1929, Chicago Great Western (CGW) debuted its *Bluebird*, a three-section articulated rail car. True high-speed internal combustion trains had first emerged in Germany in 1932 when Wagen und Maschinenbau AG's two-piece articulated, streamlined diesel-electric railcar debuted. After tests, it entered regular passenger service between Berlin and Hamburg on May 15, 1933. It was called *Fliegende Hamburger* ("The Flying Hamburger") and attracted worldwide attention as the fastest regularly scheduled train in the world. It operated at nearly 100 miles per hour for extended periods in regular service.

McDonald was intrigued by the prospect of a streamliner and encouraged SP's mechanical department under George McCormick to come up with a practical high-speed design. However, McDonald was more keen on improving SP's prestigious

After World War II, SP's public system schedules featured this stylized image of its *Daylight* running along the Southern California coast. Public timetables featured detailed train schedules, information on car types and services, a system map, fare information, and SP advertisements. *Author collection*

507—Southern Pacific "Daylight" Coast Line, Los Angeles to San Francisco, California

© CURT TEICH & CO., INC.

OB-H679

Southern Pacific's new streamlined *Daylight* thrilled the public. The back of this vintage postcard reads "The brightly colored, orange and red, Million Dollar Southern Pacific *Daylight* speeds daily along the magnificent California Coast line between San Francisco and Los Angeles—the route of the Missions." Pictured leading the train is GS-2 4412, one of the six original streamlined *Daylight* locomotives. *Author collection*

Coast Line than lower-profile Sacramento services. On September 26, 1933, a little more than four months after the *Fliegende Hamburger* had entered revenue service, SP's Charles L. Eggleston submitted an advanced railcar design to McDonald. According to Wright, the three-piece train would have cost $200,000. SP had consulted the Winton Engine company and, in all likelihood, the train would have been powered by either a Winton distillate engine, like Union Pacific's *Streamliner*, or by an early diesel engine like Burlington's *Zephyr*. Costs and technology aside, the design that resembled the CGWs and German railcars didn't appeal to McDonald, who commented, "The train looks more like a high-speed trolley than a streamliner." He urged further design work and stressed a luxurious streamlined train.

So, despite its pioneering look at high-speed streamlined trains, Southern Pacific lost the initiative. In 1934, Burlington and Union Pacific launched their famous streamlined internal combustion trains, and a year later Milwaukee Road's streamlined, steam-powered *Hiawatha*s were setting speed records. Thompson argues that Santa Fe's plans for diesel streamliners and an expansion of its California rail and bus services finally pushed SP to act.

SP took a conservative approach, though, and wasn't ready to fully embrace the latest technology. According to Don Hofsommer in *The Southern Pacific 1901–1985*, during March 1936, SP's executive committee finally got the ball rolling again and made plans for a plush Pullman-built streamliner to ply the rails of the California coast. George McCormick's team executed Angus McDonald's vision and contracted construction of an all-new, streamlined *Daylight*. Like the Milwaukee Road, SP relied on advanced steam power rather than innovative diesel-electric technology to haul its train, yet employed recently developed lightweight passenger car technology.

Streamlined *Daylight*

On March 21, 1937, Southern Pacific proudly launched its new streamlined *Daylight*s. Joint ceremonies at San Francisco and Los Angeles christened the trains—SP executives, movie stars, and the public joined in the celebration. The *San Francisco Chronicle*, on March 22, 1937, reported the departure of the first Los Angeles–bound streamlined *Daylight*:

Southern Pacific's Pullman-built streamlined *Daylights* were among the most sophisticated modes of travel. On February 15, 1948, train 96, the Los Angeles–bound *Noon Daylight*, was seen racing along the Pajaro River through Chittenden Pass near Watsonville Junction, California. The *Daylight's* round-end observation car gave passengers a splendid view back along the line. *Fred Matthews*

Miss Lorene Dyer, daughter of J. H. Dyer, vice president in charge of operations for the company, was the sponsor.

"I christen this beautiful train 'The Daylight.' May she have many smooth runs, on time, and may she give enjoyment and comfort to many people," she said as the bottle smashed and champagne bubbles streamed down over the brilliant red, orange and black sides of the largest streamlined steam locomotive in the world.

Meanwhile, at Central Station in Los Angeles:

Miss Olivia de Havilland, San Francisco girl who has risen to stardom in Hollywood, was christening the second of the two "Daylights" just before its departure on its first regular northward trip.

Promptly at 8:15, both here and at Los Angeles, conductors gave their "highball" signals to engineers, air horns sounded their long musical notes, and the two streamlined rail liners were off with full passenger lists, one northbound, the other heading south.

If just one image characterizes SP's late steam era it's this: East of San Jose, train 98, the *Morning Daylight*, led by *Daylight*-painted GS-4 4453, overtakes freight No. 932, led by Baldwin-built cab-ahead 4248. These locomotives represented the zenith of SP steam development; both were 12 years old when this photograph was exposed at milepost 47.3 in 1953. *Fred Matthews*

Each of the 12-car streamlined beauties cost $1 million, making them not just the most stunning and spectacular new trains in the United States, but also, by far, the most expensive. On their inaugural runs, as they rolled toward their respective destinations, national radio praised their attributes in glowing detail, allowing listeners in California and across the country to bask in the glory of SP's *Daylight*. It was a great moment for railway passengers.

Pullman and SP had worked together on the design of the cars and interior. Wright notes that SP's E. B. Dailey worked under McCormick to refine *Daylight* passenger car design. The *Daylight* blended new technologies and concepts with a conventional approach. One flaw of the early lightweight articulated trains, such as Burlington's *Zephyr* and SP's stillborn 1933 streamliner, was operational inflexibility. If one car failed, or if the power car developed difficulty, the whole train was laid up. On advice from Pullman, SP ordered pairs of articulated coaches that shared a common truck, and featured conventional end couplers. This took advantage of reduced tare weight without unnecessarily compromising flexibility. All of the *Daylight* cars used Pullman's new designs. They were lighter and featured a lower center of gravity than conventional passenger cars, allowing for faster operation through curves. *Railway Age* reported in its March 13, 1937, issue that the carbodies were made of Cor-Ten steel with welded truss-style side framing using vertical and diagonal supports. Underframes were constructed from U-center sills that extended the length of the car, while critical underframe components were made from cast steel for greater structural stability. Corrugated stainless-steel side sheathing, with a flat band in line with the windows, covered the outsides of the cars. (Ryan and Shine explain that SP's

What could be more
exhilarating than watching
the *Coast Daylight* race up
the Peninsula? In this
classic scene, Southern
Pacific GS-4 4457—the
highest number of the
class—whisks train No. 99
past the commute station at
San Bruno, just minutes
away from its destination
of San Francisco, on July
30, 1954. *Fred Matthews*

In steam days, the
Morning Daylight typically
ran with a pure set of
streamlined Pullman
equipment. On Valentine's
Day 1948, train 98 works
at Santa Margarita,
California. To the
connoisseur of luxury
travel, a romantic interlude
along the California coast
included a spin on SP's
finest. *Fred Matthews*

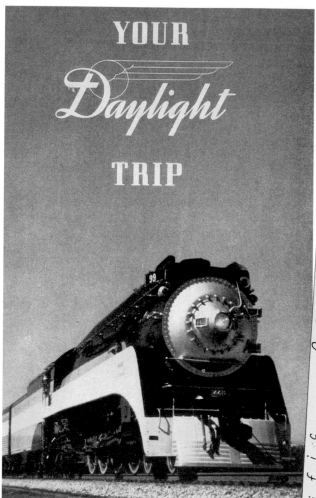

YOUR *Daylight* TRIP

Daylight passengers could learn about their journey with pocket-sized brochures that featured a stylized map and information about places of interest along the route. *Author collection*

A MAP OF YOUR COAST LINE TRIP

desire for corrugated stainless-steel siding stemmed from interest in Budd drawings. While Pullman accommodated SP's wishes, Ryan and Shine are careful to point out that on Pullman's Cor-Ten steel cars, corrugated stainless steel was strictly a cosmetic application. On Budd-built cars, corrugated shot-welded stainless steel was structurally integral to the overall design.) Part of the streamlined treatment was to cover appliances below the underframe with semi-elliptical stainless-steel sheet aprons beneath the sidesills. Pressed steel was used on car ends, while the roof was made from alloyed steel welded in place on U-type supports forming an oval profile.

The cars were painted in SP's flashy new red, orange, and black "Daylight" livery and decorated with the new stylized *Daylight* insignia designed by Charles L. Eggleston and specified by Angus McDonald. The *Daylight* livery played on colors associated with California and SP—*Daylight* orange is a near match to the hue of the California poppy and has an obvious golden connotation harking back to the gold rush.

This map of the Coast Line allowed passengers to trace their journey along the scenic California coast. SP stressed the high quality of the *Daylight* trip as well as the train itself. SP spent millions of dollars advertising and promoting its *Daylight* and this was part of the follow-through to insure passengers enjoyed their ride. *Author collection*

In their original configuration, the *Daylight* train sets were virtually identical, consisting of a 79-foot–2-inch combination coach-baggage car, a 79-foot–2-inch nonarticulated coach, and three two-section articulated coaches (each section measured 66 feet, 1 inch; total length was 132 feet, 2 inches). Toward the back were three more 79-foot–2-inch cars: a tavern, a diner, and a parlor. Bringing up the tail was a 78-foot–1-1/2-inch enclosed round-end parlor/observation car. All the cars were 10 feet wide and 13 feet, 6 inches tall.

The ends of the cars were fitted with both center and outer diaphragms, making transitions between the cars visually seamless and the whole train appear as one contiguous unit rather than separate cars.

Pullman and Southern Pacific collaborated on the cars' interior design. The result was a variety of stylish décor using subdued colors that complemented the trains' flashy exteriors. It was an Art Deco delight. Each seat had headrests with coverings displaying the *Daylight* insignia. Coaches featured extra larger-than-normal windows, 5 feet, 4 inches wide, designed to give passengers a better view from the train. A blend of soft and direct electric lighting lent a modern ambience. Secondary ceiling lighting provided a soft overall glow, while spotlights were positioned over each seat for reading and direct illumination.

The tavern car was a sophisticated rolling pub and bar. According to *Railway Age*, one end of the car was a coffee shop with a central lunch counter covered with gray Pneu-Tile supplied by Midgeley & Borrowdale of Chicago. The flooring was covered in marbled red and tan linoleum bordered by gray and black. Counter stools were

aluminum and upholstered in deep-orange leather. The swank result was conducive to conversations over black coffee, Hollywood gossip, and idle concerns over real-estate prices. More serious discussions might be held at the far end of the car in the tavern; over blended double martinis stock tips were traded, politics were discussed, and ominous events in Eastern Europe were debated in hushed whispers. The two public areas were separated by a kitchen, 15 feet long, at one end of which was a quarter-circular bar set out 6 feet, 6 inches from the wall with marquee lighting and edge-lit glass. Beyond were three sets of semicircular cocktail lounge seating designed for 18 people. Ceiling lights filtered by rotating colored gels varying from red to yellow to blue produced subtly blended and continuously changing patterns.

The dining car was divided into kitchen, pantry, and dining areas, and had seats to accommodate 40 passengers at a time. The parlor car featured a modest-sized stateroom and a much larger central section 52 feet, 5 inches long with 29 rotating chairs built by General Fireproofing of Youngstown, Ohio. Overhead lighting was indirect and carpeting was a green block pattern with swatches of coral, rust, and jade. The parlor/observation was arranged in a similar format, although the observation section featured movable furniture. Here, passengers could relax and gaze back along the tracks as the train clipped along at speed. Every so often, the *Daylight* might pass one of SP's

This carefully posed publicity shot depicts the interior of one of SP's luxurious Pullman-built tavern-lounge cars during the heyday of the Daylight. This was a time when passengers dressed up for long-distance travel, when taking the train was an event, and when riding the Daylight lent prestige and status. A trip was to be savored, and the journey there may have been just as important as the destination. What would we pay today for such luxury and class? Southern Pacific photo, Bob Morris collection

One of SP's justifications for operating deluxe passenger trains was to promote its premier freight routes. Even in their heyday, passenger trains contributed only a fraction of the revenue generated by SP's primary business—freight traffic. In 1960, SP's *Coast Daylight* rolls past the railroad's sprawling Taylor Yard in Los Angeles. By this time the classic neon insignia had been removed from the round-end observation car. *Bob Morris*

heavy freights, perhaps a fruit block heading up the coast or a train laden with sugar beets. The tavern and coffee shop were open with nonrevenue (ticketed) seating; passengers could come and go as they pleased.

Each 12-car train had capacity for 584 revenue passengers. From end to end, the trains measured 870 feet. Excluding the locomotive, each train set weighed more than 1.1 million pounds when empty. *Railway Age* estimated that this was one-third less than a conventionally designed passenger train. Further, the magazine noted that with a serviced locomotive, a *Daylight* weighed 2,028,551 pounds.

Daylight Power

Rather than delve into the realm of new diesel-electric power, SP chose proven technology. Leading each *Daylight* run was a massive, specially designed streamlined steam locomotive. The *Daylight* locomotives were some of the most handsome ever conceived. They used modern styling and highly refined, well-established steam technology that made them direct descendants of Robert Stephenson's famous *Rocket* built more than a century earlier. It had been typical policy for most American railroads to tailor locomotive designs to specific applications. In the case of the *Daylight*, Southern Pacific desired to operate its 12-car passenger trains on fast schedules with a minimum of stops. Further, they wanted to ascend numerous 1 percent grades without hesitation and assault the tortuous 2.2 percent Cuesta grade without a helper.

To meet this application, Lima Locomotive Works of Lima, Ohio, built for SP six 4-8-4s that were among the most modern locomotives of their kind delivered in late 1936 and early 1937. Lima was the smallest of the three major steam builders and in the 1920s had secured larger market share through innovation and aggressive marketing. Key to this strategy was its "Superpower" concept, through which it had developed a variety of powerful, efficient locomotives vastly superior to most previous types. These had changed the way the other builders approached locomotive building. The key to Superpower was a high-capacity boiler and ample firebox that permitted continuous high-speed, heavy-duty operation without risk of running out of steam. This, in conjunction with modern appliances, refined locomotive operation, honed performance, and improved reliability. The development of the radial four-wheel trailing truck had enabled the construction of a larger firebox and thus a bigger boiler; a Superpower type, regardless of manufacturer, is identified by its four-wheel trailing truck. The 4-8-4 type was developed in 1927 and by the mid-1930s had become one of the most popular new wheel arrangements built in North America.

Southern Pacific's six *Daylight* 4-8-4s were classed GS-2 (standing for <u>G</u>olden <u>S</u>tate and <u>G</u>eneral <u>S</u>ervice) and numbered 4410–4415. These stunning locomotives caught the eye of everyone who saw them, and were the most colorful machines to have ever graced Southern Pacific property. Unlike the early streamlined steam locomotives designed in wind tunnels and shaped to reduce wind resistance, SP's *Daylight*s were streamlined primarily to fulfill aesthetic ideals. Boiler casing enclosed the majority of the locomotive's piping, its sand domes, steam dome, smokestack, and related equipment, yet the locomotive maintained a traditional shape without an excess of gratuitous shrouding. The pilot was neatly streamlined in an angular fashion and designed to avoid interfering with the front coupler and air hoses. Neat skirting ran from pilot to cab along the running boards. The headlight was encased in the streamlined housing, centered on the smokebox door. The livery matched the *Daylight* train sets: boiler casing was glossy black; the smokebox door, marker lamps, horns, and other front-end equipment was painted aluminum; and pilot and side skirting was dressed in brilliant orange with rows of silver stripes on the pilot, mimicking a traditional lattice-style pilot used by older locomotives. A deep-red stripe ran across the midsection of the boiler. The tender carried the striping pattern that was established by the locomotive and ran throughout the passenger consist. The reciprocating parts—drivers, connecting rods, and valve gear—were made of highly polished steel. Locomotive tires and wheel rims were dressed in white.

The four pairs of drivers used modern, cast-steel Boxpok wheels—rather than the traditional spoked variety—and these measured 73 1/2 inches in diameter. The frame comprised a cast-steel bed with integral cylinders. The outside boiler diameter was 86 inches, and it was made of carbon steel and designed for 250 pounds operating pressure. Modern internal appliances included efficiency-improving devices like the Elesco Type E superheater (used to superheat steam before it entered the cylinders to produce maximum horsepower) and a Worthington feed-water heater (to minimize thermal losses when adding water from the tender to the boiler). As with the majority of SP's locomotives, the GS-2s were oil fired. Based on specifications published in the February 27, 1937, *Railway Age*, in working order, the locomotive alone weighed 448,400 pounds and placed 266,500 pounds on drivers. The tender weighed 372,880 pounds. With this

weight, tractive effort (calculated at 83 percent boiler pressure) was listed at 62,200 pounds and at 74,710 pounds when using the trailing truck booster engine (employed for starting).

The tenders had a rectangular shape designed to conform to the width and profile of the passenger cars and were carried by six-wheel trucks to better distribute their weight. The tenders carried 22,000 gallons of water and 6,275 gallons of fuel oil. "Southern Pacific Lines" was written across the side of the tender in large white serif type.

Although dressed for streamlined fast passenger service, the GS-2s were designed for dual service and were used to haul freight as well as secondary passenger trains.

Streamliner Success

Southern Pacific's brilliantly painted *Daylight*s were a gleaming success in otherwise dark and trying times. When they debuted, newspapers were rife with foreboding news. On Thursday, March 18, 1937, the *San Francisco Chronicle* detailed Germany's military spending under the headline "War Machine Second to None, Hitler's Aim." On the same page it warned of Mussolini's growing Mediterranean ambitions and its threat to Britain. Bombs were exploding in Jerusalem, and the American economy, while improving from the darkest days in 1933, was still a long way from robust. In general, railroading was in the doldrums. Hundreds of locomotives and thousands of cars were stored nationwide. Traffic, although rebounding, was still down from 1929 levels. Amid this forecast of gloom, the new *Daylight* spelled hope. A poor farmer who saw the glistening red and orange train blitz across the fields in the Salinas Valley might have thought, "At least Southern Pacific is moving forward." The businessman in San Francisco, hesitant to make the daylong journey to Los Angeles, just might have changed his mind when he heard of the *Daylight*.

Train 98 overtakes an eastward fruit block led by AC-10 cab-ahead 4222 near San Luis Obispo, California, on August 10, 1953. Fruit blocks were long freights of refrigerated boxcars, typically dressed in bright-orange paint that carried California produce from harvest to market. Passengers riding along the Coast Line would have seen a variety of SP freight, typically on sidings and out of the way of fast passenger trains like the *Coast Daylight*. *Robert A. Buck*

Thompson points out that with the streamlined *Daylight*, Southern Pacific tapped a latent travel market. SP didn't just provide transport, it encouraged travel. This image was helped by Southern Pacific's aggressive multimedia advertising. But SP didn't spend millions of dollars just to give people a morale boost—it also hoped to turn a profit with its new trains. In this regard, the *Daylight* seemed extremely successful.

In the days and weeks prior to the *Daylight*'s celebrated launch, SP filled newspapers with advertisements for the train. There was no virtue in running a stealth service. After absorbing the dire news on the front pages, readers of the March 18, 1937, *Chronicle* could find SP's large ad with headlines that jumped off the page and detailed text explaining SP's new services, including *Daylight*. Perhaps most importantly SP advertised its fares:

"Daylight" fares: Our regular coach and tourist fares to Los Angeles ($9.47 one way, $14 roundtrip) are in the streamlined chair cars on the *Daylight*. ALL CHAIR CAR SEATS MUST BE RESERVED IN ADVANCE (NO CHARGE). Chair car passengers have full access to Coffee Shop, Tavern, Diner. The two parlor cars are restricted to first class tickets ($14.20 one way, $18.75 roundtrip) plus a seat charge of $1.50 each way.

In the later diesel era, F units in SP's scarlet and gray livery were standard power on many remaining passenger trains. These views of train 98, the *Coast Daylight*, depict the locomotives being serviced en route at San Luis Obispo, California, in July 1966. Water is added for the steam boiler, and laborers take care to clean the windshields on the lead unit. *Richard Jay Solomon*

Right: Southern Pacific train staff wore specially designed uniforms with a *Daylight*-style insignia on the sleeves. An SP trainman stands on the platform at San Luis Obispo, waiting to assist passengers. *Richard Jay Solomon*

The cylinders, valve gear, driving rods, and driving wheels of a GS-4 Northern represented one of the most advanced reciprocating steam locomotive designs. The GS-4, with 80-inch driving wheels and 26x32-inch cylinders powered by a high-capacity boiler working at 300 psi, developed sufficient power to keep a 20-car *Daylight* on schedule—except for the tough climb over Cuesta, which required a helper. *Brian Solomon*

The most famous of all the *Daylight* locomotives is the legendary 4449. As the only fully streamlined SP 4-8-4 to escape scrapping, 4449 was restored to operating condition in 1974 and 1975 for work on the *American Freedom Train*, a special tour train celebrating the American Bicentennial. Although streamlined, SP's GS-4 maintained the railroad's characteristic steam-era aesthetic. There was no mistaking a Lima-built SP GS-4 for any other railroad's locomotive. The silver smokebox with twin headlights, skyline casing around the airhorn, the smokestack, and other equipment all put forward the SP look. *Brian Solomon*

Preserved Southern Pacific 4-6-2 2472 and 4-8-4 4449 lead a 1991 Sacramento Railfair excursion train along the shores of San Pablo Bay at Pinole, California. These classic locomotives inspire nostalgia for the days when SP passenger trains regularly connected California cities with those across the Southwest. *Brian Solomon*

One of the most famous profiles in American railroading, SP's GS-4 locomotive 4449, races through Hooker Creek toward Redding, California. *Brian Solomon*

The *Daylight's* competitive fares and fast 9-hour-45-minute schedule, combined with the sexy new streamlined consist, made for a winning combination. By July 1937, SP was advertising that the train had carried 62,899 passengers in its first three months and was averaging 342 passengers daily in each direction. By the end of the first full year, the *Daylight*s had carried 253,573 passengers, making it the most heavily traveled single-section train in the United States. (American railroads often operated popular services in multiple sections, each a "train" in its own right, consisting of a locomotive and cars and operating minutes apart in succession over the line on the same schedule. The rules of operation insured proper separation so that accidents would be avoided.) Occasionally, SP was compelled to run a second *Daylight* section with conventional equipment, much to the disappointment of passengers.

Within a year of *Daylight's* debut, SP was making plans for another streamliner and ordered an additional 14 Lima 4-8-4s of a refined design. These pulled 14 cars, boosting revenue seating to 639 passengers per train. SP also introduced a three-unit articulated dining car, equipment unique to the railroad. With 152 seats, this diner could accommodate almost four times as many people as the diner on the original 1937 *Daylight*. Experience with the first *Daylight* streamliners led SP to incorporate a number of minor modifications on the new trains, including the installation of luggage elevators in the parlor and chair cars to aid in loading, and garbage chutes in the kitchen and bar to alleviate the need for waste storage (chutes allowed garbage to be stored beneath the car and removed during servicing). New interior liveries were introduced, and a brightly colored, neon-lit *Daylight* insignia glowed on the tail of the round-end observation cars.

A radio commentator, describing the all-new train, days before its debut, declared it to be "The World's Most Beautiful Train," a comment that echoed SP's sentiments and has been repeated many times since. The new *Daylight* consists entered service on January 10, 1940, while the two 1937 trains were refurbished and modified to work a new Coast Line service designated the *Noon Daylight*, trains 96/97, which began operation on March 30, 1940. To avoid confusion, the early departure was redesignated the *Morning Daylight*, trains 98/99. Hofsommer notes that during the *Daylight*s' first four years, 1.3 million people rode the trains.

Minutes before it leaves for Los Angeles, train 98 readies for departure at the Third and Townsend Depot. The morning fog is burning off San Francisco Bay and it will be a nice run down the Peninsula to San Jose. The GS-4 4456, among the last of the class that retained full *Daylight* regalia, leads this morning's train. *Robert A. Buck*

On August 10, 1953, roughly 5 hours and 15 minutes after departing San Francisco, train 98 makes its station stop at San Luis Obispo. This was the halfway mark on the train's daily journey, and extra time was allowed to service the locomotives. Passengers could disembark here, stretch their legs, take in the fresh air, and, if they saw fit, make a timeless photo of the train. *Robert A. Buck*

One of the few major improvements to SP's *Daylight* trains in the 1950s was the addition of full-length dome-lounges. These "homebuilt" cars offered passengers unrivaled views of California's coast. Minutes after its departure from Third and Townsend in San Francisco, train 98 passes Potrero Tower as it enters Tunnel No. 1 on the Harriman-era Bayshore cutoff. Today, the massive concrete elevated structure supporting Interstate 280 covers the tracks here, obscuring this classic view of the San Francisco skyline. *Bob Morris*

San Joaquin Valley Services

In the early 1940s, Southern Pacific invested a further $7 million for 20 more locomotives and additional cars. This included total re-equipping of the premier San Francisco–Los Angeles overnight train, the *Lark* and equipping another whole *Daylight* train pair running via the Central Valley and Tehachapi.

According to Richard Wright, trains 51/52 began operation in 1927 as the *San Joaquin Flyer* (an older name train that previously carried the numbers 49 and 50). After 1928 it was known just as the *San Joaquin*. Following the roaring success of the coast streamliners, SP had made plans to re-equip the *San Joaquin* to provide a third daytime streamliner between the Bay Area and Los Angeles. More importantly, this train would tap the populous Central Valley and give SP a more visible presence in this lucrative traffic area.

The *San Joaquin Daylight*, operating as trains 51/52, began service on Independence Day 1941 but didn't become a full streamliner until 1942. This was a more modest train than the premier *Morning Daylight* and it typically carried a

Train 96, the *Noon Daylight*, departs Third and Townsend, San Francisco, in July 1947. The neon *Daylight* insignia at the back of the train added to the aura of modernity. This element of distinctive decor was removed in the late 1950s when SP implemented cost-cutting measures. *Fred Matthews*

combined mail and baggage car, six chair cars, a diner, a tavern car (with coffee shop), and a round-end parlor/observation. Initially, *San Joaquin Daylight* required different motive power than its coastal cousins. The Oakland–Bakersfield routing was low-grade much of the way, unlike the Coast Route, which was continuously undulating. Southern Pacific shopped three 17-year-old P-10 Class 4-6-2 Pacifics (Nos. 2484, 2485, and 2486), giving them a modest *Daylight* treatment that included the application of streamlined skyline casing on the top of the boiler to conceal the steam dome, sand dome, and smoke stack. Skirting was added to the sides, similar to that featured on the streamlined 4-8-4s. The locomotives were dressed in *Daylight* livery with "San Joaquin" painted in stylized lettering on the skirting above the cylinders. The locomotives retained their spoked drivers, traditional lattice pilot, smokebox, and Vanderbilt-style tenders. The P-10s were powerful, well-respected machines built by Baldwin. They had 73-inch driving wheels and 25x30-inch cylinders, worked at 210 pounds boiler pressure, and weighed 300,000 pounds and produced 45,850 pounds tractive effort. Although colorful and suited to the service, the *Daylight* P-10s were not given nearly as elaborate a treatment as SP had given three P-6s rebuilt for the Texas *Sunbeam* (see Chapter 3).

In contrast to the relatively easy Valley run, the run over the Tehachapis was among the toughest on all of the SP. For heavy mountain service between Bakersfield and Los Angeles, SP gave five MT-4 Mountain types a subdued *Daylight* treatment. The 4-8-2 Mountain was well suited to the rigors of the Tehachapis. The Mountain type was in essence an expansion of the 4-6-2 Pacific, having a slightly larger boiler and using four sets of drivers instead of three. The MT-4s were built at SP's own Sacramento Shops between 1925 and 1929, and featured 73-inch drivers, 28x30-inch cylinders, and 210 pounds of boiler pressure. They were significantly heavier than the P-10 Pacifics, weighing 368,000 pounds and thus applying more weight to the drivers, which gave them 57,510 pounds tractive effort. Even so, it was common practice to double-head the *San Joaquin Daylight* Mountains over the Tehachapis, either working together or with other locomotive types. The grueling Tehachapis demanded heavy power and assured a slow trip up through the sinuous rolling hills and rocky canyons that characterize this famous grade.

The scenery over the Tehachapis is sublime, and without question the highlight of a trip on the *San Joaquin Daylight,* but these mountains also represented the shortcoming of the San Joaquin route. It was longer, slower, and more costly to operate than the

Coast. However, SP was able to make up some time with fast running down the Valley, which helped offset miles of very slow track between Bakersfield and Mojave. Yet, based on the November 14, 1943, public timetable, train 52 (Los Angeles–bound *San Joaquin Daylight*) required 14 hours between terminals (including a ferry ride to San Francisco, see below) compared to 9 hours, 45 minutes for train 98.

Where the Coast *Daylight*s began their journey at Third and Townsend Streets, in the shadow of the San Francisco skyline, the *San Joaquin Daylight* started from the Oakland Mole (listed in timetables officially as the "Oakland Pier"), an antique ferry port in the East Bay. The Mole's cavernous 1882-era train shed, although comparable to big eastern terminals, was alone in the West. Screeching seagulls and deep maritime horns echoed as trains were announced over an electric public address system. SP passengers were afforded a direct ferry connection from the pier to San Francisco. Historian Fred Matthews described the Mole in the September 1994 *Passenger Train Journal* as a "Huge Cathedral of Transport." Certainly a fascinating venue for railway photographers, but not the most comforting setting for timid travelers enduring late arrivals.

This sunset view of the *San Joaquin Daylight* on the Mococo Line near Martinez, California, provides a good view of an SP streamlined articulated chair car. The two carbody sections share the center truck. *Bob Morris*

The *San Joaquin Daylight* made five intermediate passenger stops before it left the Bay Area. All told, it paused for passengers at 20 intermediate locations. After departing Oakland it followed the shores of San Pablo Bay on SP's heavily used double-track mainline toward Sacramento. At Martinez, it diverged on to the single-track Mococco Line running via Pittsburg to Tracy, California. Beginning in 1946, SP operated a section of the train from Sacramento to Los Angeles marketed as the *Sacramento Daylight*, trains 53/54. This connection consisted of just a few cars and joined trains 51/52 at Lathrop. SP's timetable advertised its "New *Sacramento Daylight* . . . No change of cars en route. The *Sacramento Daylight* operates as a unit with the *San Joaquin Daylight* between Lathrop and Los Angeles." The limited number of seats mandated a reservation requirement.

The *San Joaquin Daylight* was not the only show on the Central Valley Line. In addition, SP operated local trains 55/56 and the nightly *Owl* (trains 57/58) from Oakland to Los Angeles. While not as fast or as exclusive as the premier *Lark* (discussed below), the *Owl* was a traditional night train carrying heavyweight Pullman sleeping cars, chair cars, coaches, and a diner. Several classes of sleeping cars were available: bedroom lounge, standard sleeper, and tourist sleeper. Inaugurated in 1898, by the 1940s the *Owl* was among the oldest name trains operating on the SP. Prior to the opening of the Coast Line, the *Owl* had been an exclusive overnight train.

The Los Angeles–bound *Owl* was an early option for overnight travelers. Its ferry connection departed San Francisco at 6 p.m., with the train leaving the Mole 35 minutes later. It arrived at Los Angeles Union Passenger Terminal at a leisurely 8:35 a.m., more than 14 hours after departure. Its schedule had not been speeded up significantly in almost 50 years of operation. Like the *San Joaquin Daylight*, the *Owl* made numerous passenger stops in the Valley. If a passenger desired middle-of-the-night exercise, it paused at Bakersfield for 10 minutes at 2:45 a.m. Indeed, this was an aptly named train that gave the intrepid passenger the unusual experience of traversing the world-famous Tehachapi Loop at about 4 a.m. Dennis Ryan and

On a morning in August 1953 at Los Angeles Union Passenger Terminal, train 51, the *San Joaquin Daylight* was assigned both GS-6 4463 and Alco PA diesel-electrics. Although built after the GS-4 and GS-5s, the GS-6 was a less impressive machine as a result of World War II–era restrictions. These locomotives did not get the full streamlined treatment and possessed less impressive vital statistics. *Robert A. Buck*

At the Oakland Pier on Christmas Day 1951, the Los Angeles–bound *San Joaquin Daylight*, behind GS-6 4462, meets the incoming *Owl*, carrying heavyweight Pullmans. *Fred Matthews Sr.*

The *San Joaquin Daylight* bound for Los Angeles passes West Oakland, California, in about 1950, led by locomotive 4350, a Class MT-4 Mountain type. To the left of the train is an unusual combination of signal hardware: a traditional Union Switch & Signal lower-quadrant semaphore combined with a more modern searchlight head. The semaphore blades display "clear," meaning the track circuit ahead is unoccupied. *Fred Matthews*

In 1954, Electro-Motive built nine E9A streamlined passenger diesels for SP. These were the railroad's last new streamlined passenger power and were delivered in the classic *Daylight* livery. The E9 was powered by twin 12-567C diesel engines and produced a maximum of 2,400 horsepower. Like Electro-Motive's earlier E units, they rode on a pair of A1A trucks, which used an unpowered center axle to help distribute weight. Locomotive 6051 was preserved and restored; today it is displayed inside the California State Railroad Museum at Sacramento. *Brian Solomon*

Joseph Shine point out that the *Owl* had the distinction of being SP's last train to operate with traditional section-berth sleeping cars. Also, the train survived relatively late, as it was a workhorse for head-end traffic, carrying lots of mail and express. The train was cut from the schedule in 1965 after 67 years of service.

One of the Valley's less remarked trains was the overnight Portland, Oregon–Los Angeles *West Coast* trains 59-16/15-60. This was an unusual train because it ran via the West Valley route to Davis and then to Sacramento and on to Los Angeles via Stockton and Lathrop, bypassing the Bay Area entirely—despite its name, it never touched the coast. This was the reason for its nonstandard hyphenated numbers. Southern Pacific's train-numbering system was based on whether or not a train moved toward or away from the company's main offices in San Francisco, regardless of direction or destination. Thus, trains heading toward San Francisco carried odd numbers, while those heading away had even numbers. Since the Los Angeles–bound *West Coast* traveled toward San Francisco until it reached Davis (the junction between the West Valley Line and the "Cal-P" east–west mainline), it carried the number 15. After departing Davis, it traveled

Southern Pacific's nocturnal Oakland–to–Los Angeles run via the Central Valley was most appropriately named the *Owl*. It is seen in this time exposure at the Oakland Pier behind GS-3 4423 around 1952. The GS-3 offered nominal mechanical improvements over the successful GS-2 design. In 1949, the *Owl* departed the Oakland Pier at 9:00 p.m. and ran via Fresno and Tehachapi summit, arriving at Los Angeles Union Passenger Terminal at 10:55 the following morning. Alert passengers were treated to early morning vistas of the Tehachapi Mountains, a sublime contrast to the industrial environs of the Oakland Mole. *Fred Matthews*

away from San Francisco for the rest of its journey and thus carried the number 60. An important function of the *West Coast* was providing direct through sleeper service from Sacramento to both Los Angeles and Portland. Since the majority of SP's passenger trains to Oregon traveled via Davis and up the West Valley Line, and Bay Area to Los Angeles trains traveled either directly down the Coast Line or via Martinez and Lathrop (as previously described), the state capital of Sacramento was effectively shut out of most north–south rail traffic.

The *Lark*

The new streamlined *Lark* debuted on May 1, 1941. Despite similar styling, it was dressed in subdued two-tone gray and black livery that contrasted nicely with the brightly painted *Daylight*s. The carbodies were painted in a neutral gray, and the window section was treated with a darker bluish gray and highlighted with white pinstripes, while the roof was dressed in glossy black. Interior décor epitomized Art Deco design with stylish engraved illuminated glass panels, soft fluorescent lighting, and a mix of pastel colors. Each train carried 13 all-bedroom Pullmans, but its most stunning car was the three-segment articulated *Lark Club* dining lounge. Measuring 203 feet long, this was an elegant, sophisticated car featuring full-service railroad kitchen facilities, a dining area, half-moon bar, and lounge area. Southern Pacific advertising stated, "The lounge and dining sections are joined together by a small lobby with semi-circular seats. These seats and a circular floor pattern cleverly conceal the point of articulation.

Daylight dawns on the *Owl*. Sunrise at Tehachapi in June 1963 finds train 58, the Los Angeles–bound *Owl*, working toward the summit of the long climb from Bakersfield, California. In later years, this train operated as much to carry lucrative head-end traffic as to move passengers. A prewar articulated chair car—built for the original 1937 *Daylight*—plus a pilot tavern car and streamlined section sleeper, make up the entire passenger part of the consist. This was the last SP train to regularly carry a traditional section sleeper. *Bob Morris*

One of the few long-distance trains to northern California that did not serve the Bay Area was the Los Angeles–Portland *West Coast*, trains 15-60/59-16. This overnight run traveled south via the West Valley Line, then over to Sacramento before continuing toward Los Angeles. In this 1947 view, MT-4 Mountain-type No. 4345 splits a classic set of Union Switch & Signal lower-quadrant semaphores at milepost 96.6 in the Central Valley, railroad direction east of San Francisco, but geographically south of Sacramento. *Fred Matthews*

SP's *West Coast* as a nonstreamlined Standard Limited. On September 20, 1947, a 4300-class 4-8-2 Mountain type accelerates away from slow orders over the Highway 99 crossing in Manteca, hauling train 59, which will become train 16 upon reaching Sacramento. In SP's parlance, all odd-number trains were conceptually heading toward San Francisco, while even-numbered trains were heading away. Thus, when the *West Coast* reached Sacramento, technically its timetable direction would change.
Fred Matthews

Photographer Fred Matthews titled this image "Before Fame." In its post-*Daylight* paint, a black and silver 4449 leads the *San Joaquin Daylight* at Martinez, California. Across the platform is the Portland-bound *Cascade* with Alco PA/PB diesels. Many of the *Daylight*-dressed 4-8-4s lost their colorful livery in later years. The famous 4449 didn't regain its *Daylight* look until 1981, when it was restored for the first Sacramento Railfair.
Fred Matthews

In 1960, a trio of *Daylight*-livery Alco PAs leads train 99, the *Coast Daylight,* at Glendale, California. Southern Pacific's PA diesels were regulars on this 9-hour-45-minute run from Los Angeles to San Francisco. In 1960 the *Daylight's* passing was largely unreported. With the loss of steam still fresh in memories, diesels were seen as common and characterless. Today, thousands of people would flock to the tracks to experience the passing of a PA-powered *Daylight. Bob Morris*

The effect is that of one continuous room more than 131 feet long . . . . This wonderful expanse of pleasure-on-wheels is an exclusive with Southern Pacific."

The space flexibility of the exceptionally long *Lark Club* allowed SP to regularly seat 24 people for dinner and 56 for breakfast. The diner was decorated in green and silver, while the lounge was blue and gold. The doors of the *Lark Club* were electropneumatically operated and the windows covered with venetian blinds. Southern Pacific paid $247,000 for the car, a princely sum for a new passenger car in the early 1940s, considering SP paid $1 million for each of its original *Daylight*s.

At San Jose, an Oakland section of the *Lark* joined the main train from San Francisco. The *Lark's* round-end observation cars featured sleeping accommodations in addition to the observation lounge. Unfortunately, both of these distinctive cars were destroyed in different wrecks within a few months of the streamliner's debut.

The *Lark* cars featured smooth sides rather than the corrugated stainless steel used on the early *Daylight* cars. Typically, the train was oriented so that the *Lark Club* was

SP upgraded the *Lark*—its premier overnight train between San Francisco and Los Angeles—in 1941. It re-equipped the service with new streamlined consists that featured deluxe modern amenities. In 1948, GS-4 4447 leads train 76, the Los Angeles–bound *Lark*, toward Los Angeles Union Passenger Terminal. *Jay Williams collection*

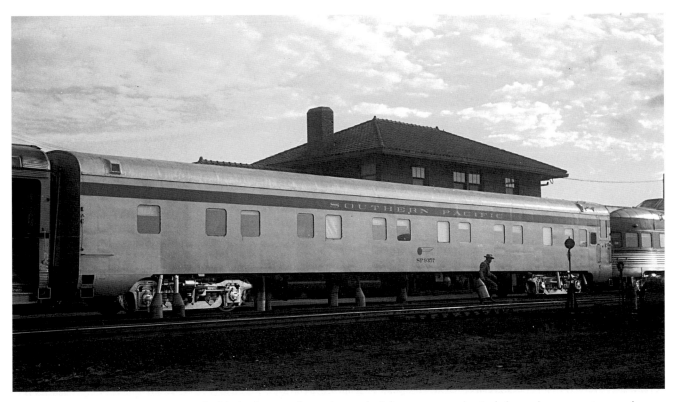

Southern Pacific car 9357 was a 13-double bedroom Pullman sleeper built for service on the *Lark*, but in later years it served on other trains as well. It is seen in SP's last long-distance passenger livery. Unlike the streamlined *Daylight*, which originally featured streamlined cars with corrugated sides, cars built for the *Lark* had smooth sides. *Otto Perry, Denver Public Library Western History Collection*

near the middle of the consist with groups of sleeping cars on both ends. This centralized the location of the train's most popular car, minimizing the distance the average passenger needed to walk to dinner.

Southern Pacific advertised "It's Smart to Ride the *Lark!*" and promoted the train along with the *Daylight*s as "One of the most beautiful trains in America." Focusing on lucrative overnight business trade, Southern Pacific continued to refine the train to make it compelling to businessmen. According to the 1946 timetable, the *Lark*s departed their respective terminals at 9 p.m. and arrived at their destinations at 9 a.m., thus giving riders a full night's sleep aboard the train with time for dinner, relaxation, and perhaps a little paperwork. In later years schedules were adjusted. The "Lark Phone," a state-of-the-art radio telephone, was installed on the *Lark Club* in 1949. SP boasted, "You can call from the *Lark Club* to any phone, anywhere in the world (even on the other *Lark*) while the train is in full flight." This was considered remarkable in an era before personal cell phones and even direct distance dialing. How many business clients were awed with a crackling call from a colleague phoning as the train rolled along the coast? The Lark Phone only lasted eight years, but it made an impression on travelers.

Super 4-8-4s

By the 1930s, modern steam locomotive design was the result of 100 years of gradual refinements to the basic reciprocating engine. Engineers were continually seeking ways to improve both performance and efficiency. When SP ordered its second batch of 4-8-4s from Lima in late 1937, Lima made them even better than the first batch. These 14 locomotives, designated GS-3, appeared very similar to the GS-2s but featured several significant improvements. Driving-wheel size was increased to 80 inches to allow for smoother running at high speeds. Also, there was nominal adjustment in cylinder dimensions, increasing the bore and decreasing the stroke to yield 26x32-inch cylinders. Locomotive weight was also increased by 11,600 pounds, resulting in a slightly greater tractive effort of 62,800 pounds without booster, 75,000 pounds with. According to the July 1938 *Railway Mechanical Engineer*, the driving wheelbase was lengthened by 18 inches to 21 feet, 6 inches, and the total engine wheelbase was increased by 22 inches to 47 feet, 8 inches. While boiler dimensions were essentially the same as the GS-2, the GS-3's boiler shell and crown sheet were made of alloyed nickel steel instead of open-hearth carbon steel. This made the boiler significantly stronger, allowing an increase in boiler pressure to 280 psi.

The zenith of the SP's Northerns—and the definitive *Daylight* locomotives—were the GS-4s built in 1941. These 28 locomotives were numbered 4430 to 4457, and like the GS-3s featured 26x32-inch cylinders and 80-inch drivers; however they were 15,000 pounds heavier, operated at 300 psi boiler pressure, and produced 78,650 pounds tractive effort (with booster). They looked more impressive, too, and featured a

On a bright morning in 1962, the San Francisco–bound *Lark* exits Tunnel No. 3 on the Bayshore cutoff within the city of San Francisco. As late as 1958, train 75 was scheduled to carry 17 cars between Los Angeles and San Jose, including three for head-end shipments, two chair cars, and a snack lounge (remnants of the *Starlight*), eight standard sleepers, and a three-section articulated lounge-diner-kitchen. Two of the sleepers were destined for Oakland and were separated from the main train at San Jose. *Bob Morris*

Nearing the end of its six-decade career, the *Lark* passes Potrero Tower on its approach to the Third and Townsend Depot in San Francisco. The train's consist is a hodgepodge of SP streamlined equipment, much of which had originally been ordered for other name trains. SP's late-era operations mixed and matched cars as needed with little consideration for the equipment's heritage or livery. The *Lark* made its final runs on April 7, 1968. *Bob Morris*

distinctive dual-headlight arrangement that included both a sealed twin-beam high-light and an oscillating headlight.

In 1941, Lima Locomotive advertised the latest batch of "Super-Power" it had built for SP: "The Locomotives will be used to power the new 'Overnight' passenger trains that the Railroad had inaugurated between San Francisco and Los Angeles as well as the famous 'Daylight' trains between the two cities. In addition to passenger service, these locomotives will also be used to power the overnight 'Hotshot' freight

Overnight passenger trains typically carried lots of head-end traffic, which greatly contributed to revenues. In 1963, the Oakland–Los Angeles *Owl* is seen behind three SP Electro-Motive–built F units near the famous Tehachapi Loop, high in the Tehachapi range outside Keene, California. Three classic heavyweight baggage cars are followed by a railway post office and the first of the streamlined passenger cars. *Bob Morris*

that the Southern Pacific has so successfully been using to reclaim LCL [less than carload] freight."

The flashy million-dollar passenger trains and state-of-the-art steam locomotives were all part of SP's marketing scheme to win both passengers and freight back to the rails. Faster luxury trains, and "redball" freights on fast overnight schedules were needed to compete with growing highway transport that had been made possible by enormous state and federal investment in new roads.

Locomotive 4449 is the most famous of the GS-4s, not because of its service record, but because it was the only one of the original *Daylight* Northerns to escape scrapping. Thankfully, it was preserved in a park in Portland, Oregon, for many years before being restored to service in the 1970s. (Another SP 4-8-4, GS-6 4460, was also preserved.) SP 4449 has come to symbolize the *Daylight* and has introduced

In their last decade, SP's long-distance trains were characterized by clean but relatively Spartan consists, as evidenced by this 1968 image of the *Coast Daylight* near San Jose, California. The famous orange and red livery has given way to the simpler silver and red paint scheme introduced with the streamlined *Sunset Limited* in 1950. *Bob Morris*

thousands to Southern Pacific and the past glory of its once great streamlined passenger services. In 1942, SP took delivery of two GS-5s; these were nearly identical to the GS-4s, except they were slightly heavier and equipped with roller bearings.

During World War II, SP received its last new passenger locomotives in the form of 10 GS-6s built by Lima. The War Production Board had strict regulations on locomotive design and the allocation of materials, so these locomotives were less impressive visually and mechanically than the earlier 4-8-4s. While still semi-streamlined, they embodied a more conservative appearance and were dressed in black paint instead of

These 1968 views by expert photographer Bob Morris capture the San Francisco–bound *Coast Daylight* running along the Pajaro River near Chittenden Pass. To replace its worn-out fleet of Alco PAs and Electro-Motive E units, SP ordered 10 SDP45s from Electro-Motive. These were a simple adaptation of the successful SD45 freight diesel and featured requisite passenger appliances such as a steam boiler for train heat. Built in 1967, the SDP45s were numbered 3200 to 3209. They weighed 410,230 pounds, about the same as a standard SP SD45, and were rated at 3,600 horsepower, enough to handle most late-era passenger consists. *Bob Morris*

bright *Daylight* colors. Their specifications were closer to the GS-2s than the GS-4s. Southern Pacific had hoped to receive 16 of these locomotives, but SP competitor, Western Pacific was allocated six of the order.

The *Daylight* 4-8-4s, along with other passenger power, were stabled on the San Francisco end of the Coast Line at Mission Bay Roundhouse, situated east of Potrero Tower, geographically south of the Third and Townsend Depot. Here, the locomotives were serviced and maintained between runs.

Relative Success

By Southern Pacific's own accounting methods the streamlined *Daylight*s turned a good profit in their first decade. In 1950, the Coverdale & Colpitts published detailed financial information that painted a rosy picture for SP. The engineering consulting firm detailed several famous SP trains, including the *Morning Daylight, Lark, San Joaquin Daylight,* and Houston–Dallas *Sunbeam*s.

Looking at the *Morning Daylight* figures for the year ending December 31, 1948, total gross revenue for the train (including passenger revenue from coaches, parlor cars, and sleepers, plus Pullman contract revenue and head-end revenue from mail, express, and baggage) was $2,973,930. Train expenses—crew wages, fuel, lubricants, train supplies and expenses, power plant maintenance, train maintenance, and miscellaneous—were reported as $1,182,275. In addition, there was a net loss of $191,625 from the operation of dining-car and buffet services. (By this time dining-car losses were a normal part of operating expenses and justified as an expected service to passengers.) Total expenses, including those from the dining car and buffet, were calculated at $1,373,900, leaving SP with $1,600,030 in net revenue, calculated as $4.65 per train-mile.

Final analysis of a train's financial performance is not simple. Thompson suggests that most American railroads did not understand the true costs of passenger operations and even during the heyday of the new streamliners, when SP was counting *Daylight* revenue and calculating a profit, in reality the train may have

actually been losing money. Consider that in addition to being among the most expensive trains of their day, the *Daylight*s had extremely high operating costs. Each run required 45 operating personnel. Thompson asserts that the formulas that SP (and other railroads) used to determine passenger operating costs were too low. What was especially difficult was delineating the ratio of resources to support freight traffic versus passenger traffic. Also, while some trains such as the *Daylight* were reported to be very profitable, other trains were routine money losers. But simply looking at revenue and expense sheets, or trying to reconfigure operating formulas, could only tell part of the passenger story; since the turn of the century railroad management had acknowledged secondary benefits to providing luxury passenger services.

Among the benefits of the *Daylight*s most difficult to assess was the positive impression it made on the public and business. From its beginning, the streamlined *Daylight* was positioned as a strategic public relations tool. SP used the train to pacify the public, promote its lucrative freight services, and demonstrate the company's progressive intentions. With the *Daylight*, SP showed that it was forward-thinking, sophisticated, and modern. Every day, it sent some of the world's most glamorous trains up and down the California coast. The *Daylight*s were like very expensive jewelry. Regardless of cost analysis, these rolling public relation machines were contributing to the bottom line.

Imperiling the *Daylight*s was a growing reliance on highway transport. Automobile usage in California had been growing steadily since before World War I. The writing was on the wall even as the *Daylight* debuted. On Sunday, March 21, 1937, the train's first passengers could have read in the *San Francisco Chronicle*'s business section a short article titled "Record Auto Train Load Claimed," which foretold as much about the future of American railroading as it did about growing auto usage. "What is said to be the first solid trainload of automobiles brought across the country since the early years of the Depression," the article stated, "arrived in northern California yesterday for distribution to Lincoln Zephyr dealers."

Perhaps the greatest irony of all was that this announcement, like those continually beaming about the *Daylight*, came from the offices of Southern Pacific.

Southern Pacific's second order for streamlined 4-8-4s looked very much like the first. The GS-3s, numbered from 4416 to 4429, had 80-inch driving wheels compared with the 73-inch drivers of the GS-2s. They also weighed several tons more and were generally more refined. On a 1951 evening, GS-3 4423 pauses with the *West Coast* at Sacramento. *Fred Matthews*

In the summer of 1947, the Los Angeles–bound *Lark* passes Union Switch & Signal two-aspect lower-quadrant semaphores with Style-B base-of-mast mechanisms on the Coast Line near Carpinteria, California. Leading this morning's train is GS-5 4459, one of two built. The essential characteristics that differentiated GS-5s (built in 1942) from the more common GS-4s (built in 1941) was the use of roller bearings and, consequentially, their slightly greater weight. According to the late Guy Dunscomb, a renowned SP steam expert, they were SP's heaviest 4-8-4s. *Fred Matthews*

Starlight

Ridership on the Coast Route declined after the World War II boom. In 1949 SP reorganized its schedules, discontinuing the *Noon Daylight* and installing a San Francisco–Los Angeles night coach train called the *Starlight* (trains 94/95) on October 2, 1949. This was a streamlined overnight train aimed at budget travelers. Instead of conventional sleepers, passengers slept in reclining-chair car seats. According to Harry Stegmaier in *Southern Pacific Passenger Consists and Cars 1955–1958*, Southern Pacific introduced this service based on the success of similar overnight coach trains like

Pennsylvania's New York–Chicago *Trail Blazer*. The *Starlight* departed prior to the *Lark*, offering passengers an early arrival time, typically by 7:00 a.m. Stagmeier also notes that one of the special features of the *Starlight* was its all-night tavern-lounge car; most other trains closed their service cars for a portion of the journey. It would seem that the *Starlight* was aimed at revelers with lots of stamina.

Southern Pacific Commutes

For many years Southern Pacific operated the only intensive suburban passenger service in the West. Eastern railroads tended to call their suburban services "commuter

Above: Although it was SP's oldest name train, the San Francisco–Pacific Grove *Del Monte* was among the railroad's least remarked long-distance services. This train covered 124 miles in just over 3 hours, while making stops at a variety of local stations en route. It diverged from the Coast Line at Castroville in order to reach Del Monte, Monterey, and its terminus at Pacific Grove. Three-car train 141, led by one of SP's passenger service GP9s, approaches Third and Townsend in San Francisco in 1970. *Bob Morris*

Left: Southern Pacific E9 6051, dressed in the modern scarlet and gray livery, leads train 98, the *Coast Daylight*, near Brisbane, a few miles south of San Francisco, California, in 1964. By this time, the days of 20-car *Daylight* consists were a memory. In another seven years, the advent of Amtrak would mark the end of SP's *Daylight* and the luxury of long-distance passenger service through to San Francisco. Fortunately, locomotive 6051 was preserved and again wears the classic *Daylight* livery (see photo on page 52). *Bob Morris*

trains," but SP's were always known as "commutes." These operated in the heavily populated peninsula between San Francisco and San Jose. As with most suburban services these trains catered to workers traveling to San Francisco in the morning and back home in the evening. Typically, daily passengers who ride on weekly or monthly tickets and make the same roundtrip repeatedly over a moderate distance characterize commuter rail traffic. Commuter passengers have different needs than long-distance travelers. Where long-distance passengers require help with trip planning and moving lots of luggage, and demand and pay for extra amenities such as a dining service, roomier seats, and comfortable parlor cars and lounges, commuters pay for low-cost, clean and comfortable trains that run at the same time every day. Where long-distance services stop at major stations, often running for miles without a pause for passengers, commuter trains make numerous pickups at small stations.

The engineering highlight of Southern Pacific's original San Francisco–Los Angeles route was William Hood's famous Tehachapi Loop, where the line makes a full spiral in order to maintain a steady grade while ascending the mountains. This view looking toward Bakersfield depicts two passenger trains. *Author collection*

Southern Pacific developed its Peninsula commute traffic in the 1890s. Under E. H. Harriman, SP invested heavily in this route, building the Bayshore Cutoff, a 10-mile line relocation that used a network of major fills and cuts and several tunnels to greatly shorten and improve SP's access to San Francisco. Work began in 1904 and was completed roughly two years later. This entirely double-tracked line eliminated several serious grades and long stretches of street-running in San Francisco. Provision was made for additional tracks on the new cutoff and SP variously considered electrifying the line when that was a popular solution for suburban services.

SP's diesel-era *Daylight* brochure featured E9 6050, the first in the class. *Author collection*

Although SP conveyed its long-distance services to Amtrak on May 1, 1971, it continued to maintain a few passenger cars for use on business trains. On March 27, 1993, this company executive train could pass as a modern-day *Daylight* as it ascends Cuesta en route from Phoenix, Arizona, to the Bay Area. *Brian Solomon*

By the 1920s, SP was operating 24 weekday San Francisco–San Jose roundtrips. Historically, the Peninsula commutes were important to SP, in part because many of the railroad's executives lived along the line and regularly used the service. During the mid-1950s the San Francisco parade caught notice because it was one of the last intensive applications of big steam power for passenger service in the West. As SP's new diesels bumped 4-6-2 Pacifics, and later 4-8-2 Mountain types and modern GS Class 4-8-4s, from named passenger trains, these big steam locomotives were assigned to commute service. The afternoon parade at Third and Townsend in San Francisco was the last hurrah for some of SP's finest locomotives.

Following the demise of steam, SP assigned its fleet of distinctive Fairbanks-Morse (F-M) H24-66 Trainmasters on Peninsula commutes, along with steam generator–equipped GP9s and a pair of SD9s outfitted for passenger service. The Trainmasters were rated at 2,400 horsepower, making them by far the most powerful diesel-electrics on the market in the mid-1950s, well suited to meeting the commutes' rigorous schedules. A generation after steam had passed, SP's Trainmasters warranted attention as the last bastions for F-M power on a Class 1 railroad in the West. F-M had basically exited the American diesel locomotive business in the mid-1950s when the company decided it could not compete with the giant Electro-Motive Division. In 1973, SP's fleet of 20-cylinder SDP45s, bumped from long-distance passenger duties, began to replace the aging Trainmasters. After Amtrak assumed long-distance services, the commutes were SP's only passenger trains.

SP commutes were a significant early application of double-decked suburban equipment. In 1955, SP supplemented its fleet of Harriman-era commute coaches with new double-deck "gallery" cars from Pullman-Standard. Each was 15 feet, 8 inches tall and 85 feet long and had a passenger-carrying capacity of 145 passengers. Additional

In 1949, Southern Pacific replaced the *Noon Daylight* with an overnight coach train appropriately called the *Starlight*. *Southern Pacific advertisement, author collection*

IT'S NEW! BEGINNING OCTOBER 2...

The Starlight

NIGHTLY COACH STREAMLINER SAN FRANCISCO - LOS ANGELES

The new, overnight "fun train" between San Francisco and Los Angeles. It's a swift, new, streamlined service, just like the *Daylights*, only at night. And what a bargain! Only $7.50 one way, $13.50 round-trip* (plus tax) in a soft, foam-rubber reclining chair car seat, reserved just for you. No meals to buy enroute. You leave after dinner, arrive before breakfast. Only 10½ hours enroute.

The *Starlight* will carry a Tavern Car (remaining open after serving hours as a lounge car) and a Lounge Snack Car which will be open all night for cards, coffee, sandwiches and light refreshments. A Parlor Car (at somewhat higher fare). Train Passenger Agent will be at your service. Each passenger will have an individual reading lamp. Chair car lights subdued for sleeping. Special Car for women with children.

Enroute you'll read, sleep, stroll to snack bar or Tavern, meet new friends, enjoy the thrill of nighttime scenery — sleeping towns, the dark shapes of mountains, the glow of stars or moonlight on Pacific Surf.

By *Starlight*, you'll save all the precious daytime hours on your pleasure or business trip. Perfect with children—each gets a reserved seat without cost, whether he's free (5 through 11), or full fare. All seats reserved but *no seat charge*. Reserve now!

The *Starlight* schedule: Leave San Francisco and Los Angeles at 8:15 p.m., arrive at 6:45 a.m. Northbound *Starlight* connects at San Francisco with northbound *Shasta Daylight* for Portland.

*Lowest fare one way and round-trip tickets to and from the East are good on the *Starlight*.*

ALL DIESEL POWERED Sunset Limited FASTER THAN EVER

★47 Hours Eastbound

This is the first step in our improvement program for the Sunset Limited . . . toward an entirely new 42-hour streamliner next year. Now, it's diesel powered all the way. Faster!

The Sunset Limited carries Pullmans with all types of accommodations. Reserved seat Reclining Chair Cars, Complete Lounge Car facilities for Pullman passengers. Dining Car service.

★46½ Hours Westbound

A through Pullman is carried between St. Louis and Los Angeles; also a through reserved seat Reclining Chair Car between Dallas and Los Angeles.

Travel via our Romantic Sunset Route. See picturesque New Orleans, the Bayou Country, Texas and the guest ranch and cowboy country of Southern Arizona.

IMPORTANT NOTICE—Effective October 2nd, the *Noon Daylight* between San Francisco and Los Angeles will be temporarily withdrawn during winter season. The *Coaster* discontinued. Service between Sacramento and Portland on the *West Coast* is temporarily discontinued.

B-61 (9-15-49) 115M Standard Folder—Form A—October 2, 1949—Subject to change without notice. Printed in U. S. A.

Above: The *Daylight*'s real competition was the automobile. Here's a contrast between an early-1950s Oldsmobile and a *Daylight* Pullman chair car. Despite providing high-quality service and aggressive advertising, in the end, SP couldn't compete with the heavily subsidized public highway infrastructure and the freedom the automobile offered. *Brian Solomon*

Left: Pacific 2424 leads three Harriman coaches on commute train 149 at San Jose, California, in 1946. This locomotive was among SP's older 4-6-2s Class P-1, built by Baldwin around 1907. After nearly 40 years of hard service, this solid old locomotive was assigned to Peninsula commute service. It was bumped from this duty a few years later when newer 4-8-2 Mountains and 4-8-4s were made surplus by the arrival of new diesels. *J. R. Quinn collection*

Southern Pacific's commute rush was one of the last great steam shows in the West. However, by December 1956, it, too, was on the verge of the diesel age. On Christmas Eve 1956, SP GS-4 4444 leads train 133 past Seventh and Townsend Streets, just four blocks from the bumper at SP's San Francisco terminus. *Fred Matthews*

Not all passenger trains on the Peninsula Line were regularly scheduled. Around 1955, GS-4 4440 leads a "Big Game Special" bound for Stanford Stadium in Burlingame. *Fred Matthews*

On November 21, 1953, SP GS-3 4418 leads train 114 past the famous "Palo Alto" in the California town named for this tall tree. *Fred Matthews*

cars came from American Car & Foundry. By 1969, SP had acquired 40 double-deck commute cars.

In an act of shortsighted corporate vandalism, San Francisco's gorgeous Mission Revival terminal at Third and Townsend—built in 1915 for the Panama Pacific Exposition—was demolished in the mid-1970s. A modern, characterless intermodal transit terminal now stands at Fourth and Townsend, a block further from downtown. Since that low point, things have improved dramatically. Cal-Train, a public body, assumed financial responsibility for the San Francisco-San Jose commutes in 1980, although SP remained as a contract operator for another decade. A more distinct visual change occurred in 1985 when the State of California bought a fleet of new Japanese-built, double-deck push-pull equipment and 18 F40PH diesel-electrics to replace aging

By the early 1960s, steam-hauled commutes were just a memory. In 1962, a fresh FP7A leads three Harriman coaches near Millbrae. *Bob Morris*

Fairbanks-Morse 2,400-horsepower Trainmasters proved well suited to SP commute service. These unusual opposed-piston diesels spent the better part of two decades working weekday passenger trains between San Francisco and San Jose. Train 132 departs the Third and Townsend Depot in 1968. *Bob Morris*

SP equipment. The last of SP's passenger equipment, including its fleet of Harriman-era cars were retired from service in 1986.

In the early 1990s, some commute runs were extended beyond the historic limit of San Jose to Gilroy. In addition, more trains were added between San Francisco and San Jose. Recent improvements have included adding sections of four-track mainline to allow for a greatly expanded service, complete with relatively high-speed express trains whisking passengers along the Peninsula and passing slower moving, all-stops local commutes. Modern transit connections at several stations, including downtown San Francisco and San Jose, provide a well-integrated public transit network.

On the morning of November 2, 1978, train 129 passes Oyster Point, South San Francisco, on its way to the Third and Townsend Depot. This was a typical late-era SP commute, passenger service GP9 3194 and six venerable Harriman commute coaches. *Brian Jennison*

An afternoon commute on April 5, 1985, with GP9 3195 and 1950s-era "gallery cars" passes near the location of the old Potrero Tower, which stood at the entrance to Mission Bay Yard. This location was greatly altered with the construction of the Interstate 280 freeway over the tracks. This immense highway structure provides a cathedral-like environment for making images of commutes, but also makes automobile travel much easier. *Brian Jennison*

At sunrise on October 14, 1976, an SDP45 leads train 123 at Millbrae, California. Five double-deck gallery cars and a single Harriman coach are this day's train. The first order of 10 gallery cars came from Pullman in 1955. SP took delivery of 21 additional cars a year later, these built by American Car & Foundry. A final order for nine gallery cars came from Pullman in 1969.
Brian Jennison

A San Jose–bound commute led by GP9 3196 makes its station stop at Santa Clara, California, on August 19, 1983. According to John Garmany, in the 1950s American Car & Foundry proposed building self-propelled double-decked diesel multiple units for SP's commute service. SP rejected the idea and stuck with locomotive-hauled trains. *Brian Jennison*

None-too-shabby SDP45 3202 waits to depart San Francisco with train 130 on July 10, 1974. SP's motive power was notoriously dirty in later years, but commute locomotives like this machine were kept in good shape. *Bill Dechau, Doug Eisele collection*

Four Scenic Routes

3

This 1991 image of SP's re-created *Daylight* working up the Sacramento River Canyon toward Dunsmuir makes for a timeless scene against the backdrop of Castle Crags. SP hired this *Daylight* consist to gain positive publicity following a disastrous derailment at the Cantara Loop in July 1991, when the railroad dropped a load of weed killer that leaked into the Sacramento River and killed fish for 40 miles downstream to Shasta Lake. *Brian Solomon*

Southern Pacific's Four Scenic Routes to California were its primary long-distance corridors. The Shasta Route connected the Bay Area with the Pacific Northwest, the Overland Route was the pioneering Transcontinental Railroad operated in conjunction with Union Pacific, the Sunset Route was SP's direct Los Angeles–New Orleans line, and the Golden State Route was the Los Angeles–Chicago corridor operated with Rock Island. In some places SP's routes overlapped, sharing the same lines and tracks. Each route was also a significant freight corridor, and promoting its popular named trains was a traditional way for SP to advertise its freight routes.

Each of these four routes hosted a flagship passenger train: *Shasta Limited, Overland Limited, Sunset Limited,* and *Golden State Limited.* Secondary services consisted of economy sleeper trains, "all stops" locals, and mail runs. In the golden age of railroad travel, SP's flagships were arguably the finest in the West, defining luxury travel. SP's deluxe *Limited*s were operated to serve the richest and most privileged travelers—they were the fastest and *best* way West. Ordinary travelers settled for the secondary runs.

Passenger trains, even the flagships, never contributed more than a small amount of revenue to SP's bottom line. Freight traffic was always SP's gravy train, but to the public it was the flagships that mattered most. As competition encroached on SP's empire it improved the schedules of its long-distance runs. But gradually highway and, later, airline competition took their toll on ridership and revenue. In the 1930s, SP, like most American railroads, suffered great loses. In 1936, Union Pacific pushed SP into the streamlined age with the introduction of the weekly *City of San Francisco* on the Overland Route. This articulated Winton-engined, Pullman-built lightweight train was the first such diesel train assigned to SP.

Based on the success of its the prewar intrastate *Daylight* streamliners, after World War II SP made a significant investment in deluxe streamliners for each of its Four Scenic Routes. Planning for these great new trains began in 1943 while war was still raging in Europe and the Pacific. Don Hofsommer wrote that SP's D. J. Russell believed that "from a passenger revenue standpoint," the railroad's best opportunities were "in providing luxurious coach-type trains with the most comfortable accommodations,

The *Shasta Daylight* was the last and the finest of Southern Pacific's *Daylight* trains. It debuted in 1949 using an all-new Pullman-built streamlined consist. Initially, one set of equipment operated with Electro-Motive E7s, the other with Alco-GE PA/PBs. This publicity photo was posed with the E7 set prior to inauguration of regular service. *Southern Pacific photo, Bob Morris collection*

After completion of the Natron cutoff in 1926, the old Siskiyou Line was relegated to secondary status, yet it continued to host some name passenger trains. Train 329, the *Rouge River*, operated daily between Portland and Ashland, Oregon. On a gray December morning it pauses at Medford, Oregon, behind MT-4 4358. *Fred Matthews*

low fares, reasonable dining-car prices, and with lounge and bar facilities."

Yet, even during SP's postwar optimism in the mid-1940s, Russell had a cynical outlook toward long-distance services. He predicted that sleeping-car travel would be doomed by airline competition. Initially, Russell's cautious approach took a back seat to optimism and SP made a large investment in deluxe streamlined sleepers. Russell's assessment was soon validated and SP's later-day streamliners had a short honeymoon; the last streamliner was delivered in 1950. By the mid-1950s SP's passenger business was in serious trouble. The railroad's multimillion-dollar investment in new cars and locomotives was a glorious step by a private company, if not a profitable one.

Shasta Route

In 1869—the year the Transcontinental Railroad was completed—Southern Pacific's predecessors began building north- ward through the Central Valley toward

The original SP all-rail route to Oregon included travel over the steep and winding Siskiyou Line. The grade between Ashland and Siskiyou Summit just north of the California–Oregon border was among the toughest climbs on the entire SP. Trains working toward San Francisco faced a prolonged 3 percent grade with numerous tight reverse curves. In this circa-1900 postcard view, three locomotives—two pulling and one pushing—are seen at the Dallarhide Trestle, lifting seven outside-braced wooden passenger cars toward Siskiyou Summit. *Author collection*

Oregon. By 1872, tracks reached Redding at the northern end of the Valley, but the rails ended here for more than a decade. The Panic of 1873 brought a temporary halt to many railway schemes across the country, but also at this time, SP interests had focused south and west. Interest in the Shasta Route was renewed in May 1887, when a melée for control of the Pacific Northwest was underway. In order to beat out its competition in Oregon and secure control of the region's transport, SP interests

7633. The "Old Man" of Cow Creek Canon, on S. P. Ry.—Southern Oregon.

Between Glendale and Riddle, Oregon, the Siskiyou Line passed through Cow Creek Canyon. A highlight of this rugged, mountainous gorge was the unusual rock formation known as the "Old Man" seen immediately in front of the train. This appears as the profile of a balding man with a pointed nose. *Author collection*

hastily pushed a railroad line over the rugged Siskiyou Mountains. Bowing to severe time constraints, Chief Engineer William Hood laid a cheap and reatively easy-to-build line over the mountains, but it was by no means the best, shortest, or most efficient route. This tortuous steep railroad, known as the Siskiyou Line, features sustained 3 percent grades. The steepest is the grade over the line's namesake Siskiyou Summit—cresting in a 3,108-foot-long tunnel at an elevation of 4,135 feet above sea level.

A last-spike ceremony at Ashland on December 17, 1887, marked completion of the line. Although slow and circuitous, this railroad allowed through passenger trains to connect the Bay Area to Portland, a vast improvement over earlier land transport options requiring passengers to endure a connecting stage coach between uncompleted ends of the railroad.

Difficulties on the Siskiyou Line led to serious consideration for construction of a superior Oregon mainline. Plans moved forward in the Harriman era, but legal problems stemming from Harriman's joint control of Union Pacific and Southern Pacific, plus the advent of World War I and government control of American railroads, delayed most of SP's planned improvements until 1923. In the mid-1920s SP started to build, and the new line, known as the Natron Cutoff, was finally opened in February 1926.

This line diverged from the old Siskiyou Line at Black Butte, California. Here, some 345 miles from San Francisco, Mt. Shasta rises to an elevation of 14,161 feet above sea level, looming large above the railroad. The Natron Cutoff crests at a significantly higher elevation than the Siskiyou Line—4,872 feet above sea level versus 4,135 feet—but it represented a vast transportation improvement and a feat of modern engineering. Where the ruling westbound grade on the Siskiyou was an astounding 3.3 percent, the Natron Cutoff features a comparatively mild 1.8 percent climb. The new line was also nearly 24 miles shorter than the old Siskiyou Line and removed numerous curves. These improved operating conditions allowed SP to chop nearly 4 1/2 hours from passenger schedules and operate significantly heavier freight trains. Yet, the Siskiyou Line was retained for local freight and through passenger trains to serve communities bypassed by the Cutoff.

SP 3249, a Baldwin-built 2-8-2 Mikado type, was the regular locomotive on train 327, the *Shasta*. This service operated between Grants Pass, Oregon, on the Siskiyou Line and Dunsmuir, California, with connecting service to the Bay Area. On a cold morning in December 1951, 327 makes a station stop at Hornbrook, California, a former helper station and one of many small communities with rail service along the Siskiyou Line. *Fred Matthews*

In modern times, the Shasta Route included several distinct SP mainlines. It used the double-track "Cal-P" route leaving the Bay Area toward Sacramento. Reaching Davis (milepost 76), most passenger services diverged and followed the near tangent West Valley Line via Woodland and Cortena, California, to Tehama, where this line joined the parallel East Valley Line. (Alternatively, trains could operate via Sacramento and Roseville, up the East Valley.) Between Tehama and Redding the tracks gradually rise out of the Central Valley. Beyond Redding, the line traditionally followed the Sacramento River on a winding water-level route all the way to Dunsmuir; however, in the early 1940s, a dam was built north of Redding to create Lake Shasta, forcing the relocation of the railroad. Built to modern standards, SP's new line is far superior to the old route. The two alignments rejoin 24 miles south (railroad direction west) of Dunsmuir at Delta.

Dunsmuir is a quintessential railroad town, nestled deep in the valley of the Sacramento. Here, the railroad sits at the base of the steep, tortuous grade up to Black Butte and beyond to the summit at Grass Lake. Known for its water and fishing, Dunsmuir is one of the great

On August 31, 1991, SP's re-created *Daylight* crosses the tall trestle at Redding, California, heading toward Dunsmuir and Black Butte, California. This tall bridge was built as part of the massive line relocation necessitated by the creation of Shasta Lake. The line was opened in 1942. *Brian Solomon*

railroad locations on the SP. Heading to Oregon, the tracks rise sharply out of town, past the Shasta Springs resort, and into a narrow box canyon. To escape the confines of the Sacramento, the tracks make a prolonged zigzag around the exceptionally tight Cantara Loop. Dunsmuir to Grass Lake is one of the most scenic sections of the SP—the combination of prolonged 2.2 percent grades and tight curves limits the length of freight trains and has resulted in helpers assigned railroad direction east of town.

Another highlight is SP's Cascade Crossing via Pengra Pass on the Natron Cutoff. Considerably farther north (railroad direction east) from Dunsmuir, the line runs first through the logging community of Klamath Falls, California, 100 miles beyond Dunsmuir, and then another 110 miles via Chemult, Oregon, to Cascade Summit (538 miles from San Francisco). From the summit to Oakridge the line descends though snow sheds and tunnels tracing an enormous letter "S" in the Cascade. In places near the top of the pass it is possible to see the line running farther down the valley, hundreds of feet below.

At Springfield Junction, near Eugene, Oregon, the Natron Cutoff rejoins the old Siskiyou Line. The northern terminus of the SP is at Portland, Oregon, milepost 771 from San Francisco (measured via Sacramento and the Siskiyou Line, a distance that was shortened substantially with the new construction).

Trains of the Shasta Route

Through passenger service to Oregon via the old Siskiyou Line began in 1887 with the descriptively named *Oregon Express* and *California Express*. Later, these trains were variously known as the *Shasta Express* and *Shasta Limited*. In *Some Classic Trains*, Arthur Dubin states that on January 3, 1913, SP debuted its new *Shasta Limited De Luxe*, an exclusive extra-fare train catering to the most elite of passengers for travel between San Francisco and Portland, with through cars for Seattle via Union Pacific lines. Already on an expedited schedule, this train was speeded up to a 33-hour schedule for the Panama Pacific International Exposition in 1915. The through San Francisco–Seattle cars were discontinued during World War I.

To mark the completion of its new multimillion-dollar Natron Cutoff, on April 27, 1927, SP introduced the overnight deluxe extra-fare, all-Pullman sleeper *Cascade*—named for the newly conquered range—between San Francisco and Portland (with through cars for Seattle). SP advertised the train's many special amenities, including an onboard barber, ladies' maid, bathing facilities, and dining, club, and open-end observation cars. Initially, it operated on a 23-hour-20-minute schedule. During the worst years of the Great Depression the service was downgraded and carried coaches, but in 1937 SP upgraded the *Cascade* and it resumed its all-Pullman sleeper status with its run trimmed to 19 hours, 40 minutes.

SP ran a full complement of secondary trains. The *Klamath* (trains 19/20) provided standard sleeper and coach services between San Francisco and Portland, and carried through Pullman sleepers to Seattle. The August 1946 SP public timetable advertised

An 11-car passenger train is featured along the Sacramento River at Castella, California. SP's Shasta Route was billed as the "Route of a Thousand Wonders." Among the attractions was Mt. Shasta itself, seen looming to the left. *Author collection*

1932 – Sacramento River Canyon, Shasta Springs, California.
SHASTA ROUTE, SOUTHERN PACIFIC COMPANY

Traditional passenger trains consisted of heavy wooden cars painted drab Pullman Green and hauled by polished black steam locomotives. This hand-colored postcard depicts a typical SP limited at Shasta Springs, California, about 1900. *Author collection*

In 1961, SP FP7A 6458, wearing the famous Black Widow livery, negotiates the curves near Dunsmuir, California, with Train No. 19, the *Klamath*. While the *Shasta Daylight* got all the prestige, the Oakland-Portland *Klamath* labored in relative obscurity. In later years, it primarily carried headed traffic, as evidenced in this photo. Eight baggage and mail cars are pictured; presumably the passenger cars are out of view around the corner. *Bob Morris*

The Portland-bound *Klamath* with its heavy head-end traffic passes Shasta Retreat above Dunsmuir in 1961. A heavy layer of snow covers Mt. Shasta, offering a picturesque vista for railway travelers seeking awe-inspiring scenery. The Shasta Route has long been one of SP's most scenic lines. *Bob Morris*

In summer 1962, Electro-Motive F units lead the *Klamath* through the curves at Small above Dunsmuir, California. One streamlined chair car on the rear is the only passenger accommodation. *Bob Morris*

The West Valley Line's level profile allowed for some fast running. A basic automatic block signal system with Union Switch & Signal three-aspect searchlights provided protection for following trains—especially important when operating fast passenger trains in succession. The *Klamath* was photographed here with F units near Willows, California. *Bob Morris*

dinner priced from $1.10 to $2.25, while other meals tended to be cheaper. In 1955, it departed Oakland's 16th Street Station at 8:20 p.m. and arrived in Portland at 7:55 p.m. the following evening. The famous streamliners were a great choice if you were leaving directly from Oakland, Martinez, or Davis, but if you wanted to travel to Portland from a lesser station you might have considered the *Klamath.* The *Rogue River* ran daily between Portland and Ashland over the Siskiyou Line, making more than two dozen intermediate stops, while the *Oregonian,* trains 17/18, was another overnight service between the Bay Area and Portland.

Shasta Streamliners

The flood of passenger traffic during World War II encouraged SP traffic managers to beam with optimism about the future. For the first time in decades, passenger volumes had risen dramatically. Many railroads, including SP, believed that substantial postwar investment in new passenger trains could retain high passenger volume. A 1946 editorial in *Railway Age* titled "Can Passenger Traffic Be Held?" explained:

"Passenger men are of the opinion that a substantial proportion of the available passenger traffic can be held on the rails, providing certain improvements are made. This opinion was expressed in a report submitted at a meeting of the American Association of Passenger Traffic Officers in Chicago."

The *Railway Age* article goes on to detail various types of new passenger equipment and explain the trials of the war environment, before offering some cautionary advice:

It behooves us to remember, however, that regardless of distance, perhaps our greatest advantage over the airplane, the bus and the private automobile is our practical ability to make it possible for people to spread out or move around while en route. We cannot hope to match the steamship in this respect, but our competition is greatest with the other forms of inland transport, so that it is to our own interest to provide ample passenger space and still have a capacity which, at any reasonable rate per mile, will yield a fair revenue per car mile.

Another item in *Railway Age* published the comments of Edward G. Budd, president of the Budd Company, regarding the U.S. travel market and principle modes of transport:

If each of these means of transport adequately develops its own facilities and services, there need not be ruinous competition between any. Railroads are essentially the wholesalers of passenger traffic. Airlines may be regarded as specialists, providing high speed at a price. The bus and the private automobile should largely function as feeders to the railroads and airplanes. While these fields may overlap, they need not eclipse each other.

The Shasta Route had long been one SP's best-performing passenger corridors, and in 1946 SP announced two new San Francisco–Portland services: an all-new streamlined *Shasta Daylight* and a totally re-equipped and streamlined *Cascade*. Although wartime restrictions had been eased, shortages of key materials delayed the delivery of the new trains by several years. According to John Garmany in *Southern Pacific Dieselization*, the new Electro-Motive E7 diesels ordered for the service and delivered in 1947 were temporarily assigned to SP's Los Angeles diesel pool while the passenger cars were under construction. In the May 28, 1949, *Railway Age*, SP President Armand T. Mercier explained that by spring the railroad would be receiving cars from Pullman and initially some would be used on the consist of the *Cascade* to provide a preview of the new equipment before it entered regular service. Finally, on July 10, 1949, SP debuted the newest, nicest, and the very last of its *Daylight* family—the *Shasta Daylight*.

The *Shasta Daylight*'s run took just over 15 hours, making it a very long daytime trip, but the fastest ever SP service between San Francisco and Portland. Klamath Falls, Oregon, was a station and service stop. The 10-minute scheduled layover gave passengers an opportunity to get off the train and stretch their legs, as seen in this August 5, 1953, view of train No. 9. *Robert A. Buck*

Detail of heavyweight business car *Oregon*, complete with *Daylight*-style insignia. *Brian Solomon*

This was a glowing example of a postwar streamliner. Southern Pacific operated a pair of nearly identical 15-car trains and ran them with diesels on 15 1/2-hour schedule between San Francisco and Portland (including ferry connection)—a full 3 hours faster than all previous schedules. The initial schedule called for an 8:10 a.m. departure from the Oakland Mole with an arrival in Portland at 11:15 p.m, a schedule designed to give passengers daytime running over the most scenic sections of the run. The September 1949 *Railway Mechanical Engineer* detailed the consists of the new streamliner. Each train had a combination baggage-railway post office where the U.S. mail was collected, carried, sorted, and delivered en route; a chair car with space for an onboard news agent; four additional chair

The Portland-bound *Shasta Daylight* runs along the Carquinez Straits at Port Costa, California, near the location of the old car ferries that were needed to shuttle trains across the water to Benicia until the massive Suisun Bay Bridge was completed in 1930. In the late 1950s, cost-cutting imposed austere styling on SP's long-distance trains, including introduction of standard simplified liveries, exemplified by the scarlet and red scheme on the Alco PAs and the silver with red stripe scheme pictured on some of the passenger cars. A few cars in the train still display the older *Daylight* scheme. *Bob Morris*

cars, one of which had quarters for dining-car staff; a three-section articulated diner, kitchen, and coffee shop similar to that installed on the 1940 *Daylight*; three more chair cars; a tavern car; and a parlor/observation car at the rear. While the parlor/observations were older cars remodeled for *Shasta Daylight* service, the rest of the consist was built new by Pullman-Standard. Instead of steel alloys, these cars used aluminum alloys for the superstructure. The underframes were made of steel, as were trucks, wheels, and other running gear. The aluminum superstructure, according to the *Railway Mechanical Engineer*, resulted in weight savings of about 5,300 pounds per car, making the whole train about 40 tons lighter than one of comparative alloy-steel construction. The typical 85-foot chair cars built for *Shasta Daylight* weighed 123,800 pounds (scale weight without passengers). The theory was that lower tare weight would result in lower operating costs. The basic train was designed to carry 442 seated passengers, 22 riding in the parlor car.

More significant to passengers than the particulars of superstructure construction were *Shasta Daylight*'s "Skyline" windows, reportedly 30 percent larger than those normally used. The Shasta Route was sold on its scenery, and *Shasta Daylight* was billed as the "'Million Dollar Train' with the million dollar view." From waterfront views

Dinner on the *Shasta Daylight* was a classy experience as portrayed in this circa 1949 publicity photo. Although SP lost money on dining cars, through the early 1950s management believed a first-class dining-car service was sufficiently important to warrant operation at a deficit. In the D. J. Russell era this philosophy was compromised and economy measures were introduced. *Southern Pacific photo, Bob Morris collection*

In the first week of July 1949, SP displayed the new *Shasta Daylight* train complete with Electro-Motive E7s at 1st and Broadway in Oakland, California. Although this streamliner served Oakland, it wasn't until Amtrak that through service from Oregon would regularly grace the tracks here at Jack London Square. The *Shasta Daylight*, like the majority of SP's Oregon trains, traditionally terminated at the Oakland Pier. The E units didn't last long on the *Shasta Daylight* and were quickly reassigned to other name trains. They were replaced by the PAs, which had dynamic brakes and were better pullers in graded territory. *Fred Matthews*

It's the summer of 1948, and all seems right in the world, at least for those witnessing the dramatic departure of the coach section of SP's *Beaver*, train 1-14, at Oakland's 16th Street Station. World War II–era GS-6 4461 blackens the afternoon sky as it marches out of town with a long train of heavyweight cars. In later years, when 4449 made appearances in the Bay Area, it needed an exemption from the Bay Area Air Quality Management District, as its smoke plumes may have violated California's strict antipollution standards. *Fred Matthews*

These interior views of an SP "homebuilt" dome-lounge depict the unusual arrangement of elevated seating at one end and an open gallery at the other. SP's domes were among the most unusual passenger cars on the railroad and distinctive from all other North American dome cars. Seven were built and from the mid-1950s were assigned to the *Shasta Daylight, Coast Daylight,* and *San Joaquin Daylight.* Cars 3605 and 3606 were often assigned to the *Shasta Daylight. Southern Pacific photos, Bob Morris collection*

On a bright morning at Martinez, California, the eastward *Senator* to Sacramento meets the streamlined *Cascade* from Portland, Oregon. A mixture of streamlined cars, including a Pullman sleeper painted for the *Sunset Limited*, make up the *Cascade*. The contrast between these two trains portrays SP's passenger services in transition. SP wasn't interested in medium-distance trains like the *Senator*, which continued with heavyweight cars and 30-year-old steam power for several years after the railroad invested in new diesel-hauled streamlined consists for its premier limiteds. *Fred Matthews*

across San Pablo Bay to the lush scenery of the Sacramento River Valley, spectacular vistas of Mt. Shasta with mist rising from its ominous volcanic cone, and the dramatic descent of the Oregon Cascades, few passengers could be disappointed by the *Shasta Daylight*'s panoramic offerings.

Electro-Motive E7 diesels were the original choice to haul the *Shasta Daylight*. Electro-Motive built and specially painted E7s with *Shasta Daylight* insignia and front-end medallions. Garmany explains that the insignia were removed when the locomotives were assigned to Los Angeles before the arrival of the *Shasta Daylight* equipment. On its inauguration, the diesel assignment for *Shasta Daylight* was split between a three-unit set of E7s and three-unit Alco PA/PBs. Numerous early publicity photos were posed with the resplendent E7s. Although Electro-Motive's E units were by far the most widely sold passenger diesels in the early days of dieselization (more than 1,200 were built between 1937 and 1964) Southern Pacific found that they were not as well suited to the rigors of mountain operation as Alco's PA/PB diesels. The Alcos were generally preferred for passenger work on the Shasta and Overland Routes, and in later years SP assigned Electro-Motive four-axle FP7s to these routes.

Southern Pacific made its last major improvement to its *Daylight* trains with the introduction of full-length dome-lounge cars in 1954. These cars were different from most dome cars on American lines. In addition to an elevated seating section where passengers could better take in the scenery, the dome also covered a nonelevated open

Three new Alco PAs lead the *Cascade* away from 16th Street Station in July 1948. Heavyweight Pullman *Glen Mawr* brings up the rear of the 15-car train. One streamlined car toward the middle of the train is mixed with 14 old heavyweight cars. The latticework masts to the right of the train are left over from SP's suburban electric operation, discontinued prior to World War II. *Fred Matthews*

In July 1948, brand-new Alco-GE PA-1 diesel-electrics contrast with the standard heavyweight Pullmans they are hauling on train No. 10, the *Cascade*, seen at Oakland's 16th Street Station. Southern Pacific was unusual in its motive power assignments—for several years, diesels with heavyweights and streamlined steam with modern lightweight cars ran side by side. Another two years would pass before the *Cascade*'s streamlined consist was introduced. *Fred Matthews*

The *Klamath* crosses Shasta Lake near Lakehead, California, with one of SP's prewar articulated chair cars, plus a heavyweight observation providing passenger accommodations. Originally designed for the *Daylight*, in later years the articulated cars were assigned to a variety of secondary trains. *Bob Morris*

area with a bar. This made for an unusually tall and bright ceiling, giving a cathedral-like effect not normally found on a railway passenger car. According to 1954's *Railway Locomotive and Cars*, SP built the cars with two variations: one with coach and lounge seating on the elevated section and another that used the elevated section just for lounge seating. The lounge sections featured sofas for passenger comfort. Maurice Sands, a California interior decorator, was responsible for the car's décor, which featured grayish, moss-green walls, jade-green upholstered seats, light-green lounge sofas, and Parkwood and rattan paneling.

In manufacturing its domes, SP started with existing lightweight cars and ordered the dome components from the Budd Company. The dome section measured 73 feet,

Southern Pacific Class GS-6 never wore orange and red paint; rather, these were the wartime utility models built by Lima in 1943 when conservation was the order of the day, including paint. They were delivered with 73-inch drivers instead of the 80-inch drivers used on the GS-3, GS-4, and GS-5. Here, 4461 leads train 15, the *West Coast*, toward a 7:35 a.m. arrival at Klamath Falls, where it will pause for 20 minutes to load and unload the contents of its many head-end cars. *Fred Matthews*

When diesels came to the *Overland* in about 1952, they were almost always Alco PAs in *Daylight* dress. The scarlet and gray livery of 1958 signaled austerity for SP's passenger business. In 1957, the eastbound *Overland* accelerates around the curve in West Oakland between stations at the Pier and 16th Street. *Fred Matthews*

Along the north face of Mt. Judah—named for T. D. Judah, who surveyed the railroad's legendary mountain crossing—modern-day concrete snow sheds protect the original 1868 alignment. SP, in its cost-cutting wisdom of the 1990s, abandoned this line in favor of the 1920s tunnel beneath the mountain. Fewer passenger trains and declining freight traffic led SP to remove portions of Donner's double track. *Brian Solomon*

7189. Cape Horn and American River, Calif., Ogden Route, So. Pacific R.R.

One of the most dramatic views on Donner Pass was at Cape Horn, east of Colfax, where the railroad was cut into a narrow ledge on the side of a cliff, hundreds of feet above the North Fork of the American River. A short midday westward passenger train is pictured along the Cape Horn retaining wall. To accommodate double track, a pair of sequential tunnels were bored inside the mountain parallel to the original alignment. In modern times, most westward trains use the newer line. *Author collection*

101

7183. In the Snow Sheds, Sierra
Mountains, So. Pacific R. R.

4 3/8 inches long and was shipped partially disassembled from Philadelphia. Since these dome-lounges were designed to operate with other cars, they were not built with vestibules or side doors. A total of seven were built.

The introduction of the *Shasta Daylight* was part of a larger reconfiguration of SP's long-distance schedules. With the same timetable change, SP canceled the *Beaver* (trains 13/14). According to the June 8, 1940, *Railway Age*, the *Beaver* was introduced as a seasonal economy streamlined train carrying air-conditioned chair cars and tourist Pullman sleepers, as well as a lounge and diner. Although it had a few streamlined cars, the majority of the train normally consisted of traditional heavyweight equipment.

Streamlined *Cascade*

A little more than a year after the *Shasta Daylight* debuted, SP introduced its new streamlined *Cascade*, an all-Pullman luxury sleeper patterned after the 1941 streamlined *Lark*. The *Cascade* was designed to appeal to business travelers and other upscale overnight clients. It carried eight Pullman sleepers and featured a distinctive three-section articulated diner-kitchen car-club very similar to the *Lark Club* and aptly named the *Cascade Club*. The exterior of the train was two-tone gray with silver, like the train's prototype. Interior décor was designed to reflect the scenic splendor of the Shasta Route. On its 1950 schedule, the *Cascade* operated on a slightly less demanding timetable, an hour slower than the *Shasta Daylight*, yet was the fastest overnight train ever operated between San Francisco (Oakland) and Portland. Its schedule was two hours faster than Amtrak's present day *Coast Starlight*, which follows much of the same basic routing, save for using the East Valley via Sacramento rather than the more direct West Valley.

Overland Route

In the 1850s, the prospect of a railroad connecting California with the East seemed absurd. Not only did nearly 2,000 miles of sparsely populated prairie, desert, and wasteland separate Sacramento and any place remotely considered civilized, but the mighty

Theodore D. Judah surveyed the line over Donner Pass during relatively dry years and miscalculated the serious effects of the region's unusually heavy snow. To keep the line passable in winter, snow sheds were built in areas of heaviest snowfall. Operating through Donner's 30-plus miles of wooden snow sheds was colloquially known as "railroading in a barn." Single track in the sheds made for some very challenging operations. In the 1920s, double-tracking on Donner eliminated many sheds. The development of cab-ahead steam locomotives was intended to alleviate problems with potential crew asphyxiation in locomotive cabs as a result of heavy working in snow shed territory. *Author collection*

Great Salt Lake Cut Off, Utah.

The back of this hand-colored postcard reads: 'The Great Salt Lake Cut-Off extends from Ogden to Lucin a distance of 102.9 miles, crossing over the north end of the Great Salt Lake. It was finished Nov. 12, 1903 after 1 1/2 half years of effort at a cost of $4,500,000.00. It saves for the S.P.R.R. Co, 43.8 miles of distance, 3,919 degrees of curvature and 1515 feet of grade." *Author collection*

This heavily retouched hand-colored postcard portrays the deluxe *Overland Limited* crossing the Lucin Cutoff at Midlake, Utah. Sunset and clouds have been added for effect. This was SP's premier Overland Route train and was typically presented in a very positive light. What could be more SP than a deluxe train rolling toward the setting sun over a multimillion-dollar infrastructure? *Author collection*

480—Sunset and Overland Limited, Midlake, Utah.

Sierra Nevada Mountains presented a seemingly impenetrable rocky barrier. Traveling overland to California was a long, arduous, and dangerous journey. The preferred route to go was via ship, either all the way around Cape Horn at the tip of South America or in combination with a land trip across Nicaragua or the Isthmus of Panama. These routes also had their perils, not the least of which were mosquitoes and the dreaded yellow fever.

But thanks to the diligent efforts of visionary railroad engineer Theodore D. Judah, a railroad *was* built to California. In addition to his early surveys, Judah organized investors and traveled repeatedly to Washington, D.C., to lobby Congress and President Abraham Lincoln to support the construction of the line through passage of the Pacific Railroad Acts. This first transcontinental line—completed on

May 10, 1869, with the famous Golden Spike celebration at Promontory, Utah—became known as the Overland Route after the famous wagon trail of the same name. It was originally operated by Central Pacific and Union Pacific, to the former of which became a key component of Southern Pacific's empire.

The Overland Route cut travel from the East to the West from weeks to just days. This iron path was a narrow thread of civilization connecting California with the rest of the nation. Because of it both railroads and the state of California flourished.

The most celebrated, most difficult, and by far most interesting portion of the Overland Route is its legendary crossing of California's Donner Pass—named for the ill-fated Gold Rush–era Donner Party that was trapped for months in the Sierra near

1547 - S. P. Co's. San Francisco - Overland Limited in Palisade Canyon, Nevada.

The famous *Overland Limited* negotiates Nevada's Palisade Canyon in the wooden heavyweight era. In its heyday, the *Overland* would have been the choice mode to California by wealthy and influential travelers. Its posh Palace cars were among the finest in the West. *Richard Jay Solomon collection*

517. Southern Pacific Car Transfer Steamer Solano, San Francisco, Cal.

Prior to 1930, SP ferried Overland Route passenger trains across the Carquinez Straits on specially built steamboats. Freight to the Bay Area tended to use longer, all-rail routes via Tracy, traveling over the Mococo Line or the original route via Altamont Pass. Train-ferry *Solano*, built in 1879, is seen delivering a full train across the straits. *Author collection*

Train 28, the eastward *Overland*, eases through Martinez, California, as the fireman leans from the side door to snatch train orders. In 1961, when this photo was made, timetable and train order operation was still used on SP's Overland Route, despite some locomotives, such as PA-2 6023, being equipped with train radios authorizing train movements by radio was not in accordance with the rules. The radio antenna, which resembles a wagon wheel, can be seen above the horn on 6023's cab. *Bob Morris*

what is now Truckee. The railroad over Donner rises from near sea level at Sacramento and climbs eastward into the foothills. The toughest climb begins east of Colfax. Here, the railroad drops into Ravine, rounds a sheer rock face known as Cape Horn, and climbs the 2.3 percent ruling grade (the toughest portion of the grade is in a tight horseshoe curve at Blue Cañon) all the way to the summit at Donner Pass, east of Norden. The line gains some 7,000 feet of elevation in a little more than 100 miles.

What makes Donner difficult is not just this climb but the exceptional weather endured on the pass. Recorded snowfall has exceeded 800 inches a year. To ease winter operations, Central Pacific constructed miles of wooden snow sheds at the highest elevations; at their greatest extent these reached roughly 30 miles from Blue Cañon to Andover, straddling both sides of the summit.

Under the intrepid and visionary E. H. Harriman, Donner Pass was slated for massive improvement and double-tracking. Harriman, however, died years before the project could be completed and the double-tracking was finally finished in the 1920s. Traveling by train over Donner presents some of the grandest western vistas. In Central Pacific days it was routine for trains to pause at

At first light, with the sun still below the horizon, the westward *Overland* pauses for its station stop at Reno, Nevada, in 1962. It is led by FP7A 6455, which is still wearing its as-delivered "Black Widow" paint scheme. The large plow on the front of the F unit is necessary to combat deep snow on Donner Pass. *Bob Morris*

In August 1992, restored SP P-8 Pacific 2472 leads a *Daylight* consist—working as an excursion train from Oakland to Stockton—along the shore of the Carquinez Straits near Port Costa, California. *Brian Solomon*

A Sacramento Railfair excursion along the shores of San Pablo Bay at Pinole, California, in spring 1991 is led by SP Pacific 2472 and GS-4 Northern 4449 and carries a variety of historic passenger cars. The tail car is heavyweight observation *Houston* in late-era *Sunset Limited*-inspired livery. Ahead of it is a Harriman suburban coach, typical of those used on the San Francisco—San Jose commutes. *Brian Solomon*

A classic SP image: Alco PAs with the *Overland* passing a lower-quadrant semaphore at sunset. Train 28 accelerates away from its station stop at Sacramento, California, in 1961. Soon this train will wind its way over Donner Pass. *Bob Morris*

Cape Horn and Gorge to allow passengers to disembark and take in the scenery. At places, the tracks wind along the rim of the American River Canyon, some 2,000 feet above river level. During the winter, Donner Pass appears as a wonderland where snow can be measured in feet rather than inches.

Harriman acquired Southern Pacific in 1901, and one of his primary objectives was to obtain the Central Pacific transcontinental line, which he felt was a natural extension of his Union Pacific. The Great Salt Lake presented a formidable obstacle to a short route, and plans had already been considered to bridge the lake. On March 8, 1904, 103 miles of new line opened, including 15 miles of fill and an astounding 23 miles of wooden trestle across the Great Salt Lake. This project shortened the Overland Route by 45 miles, eliminated many curves, and reduced the grade. The 1904 trestle was replaced with an earth-and-stone fill in the mid-1950s.

Trains of the Overland Route

The premier Overland Route trains traditionally carried train numbers 1 and 2, a symbolic indication of their importance to the railroad. In the nineteenth century,

957   GREAT SALT LAKE CUT-OFF AT SUNSET, GREAT SALT LAKE, UTAH

6A-H2493

The original 1936 *City of San Francisco* streamliner led by power-car M-10004 crosses the wooden trestle over the Great Salt Lake. This train had a pair of power cars, each with a 1,200-horsepower Winton diesel. Pullman built both the locomotive power cars and the articulated passenger cars. This train had 170 coach seats, plus room for 84 passengers in Pullman-operated sleeping cars. *Author collection*

the *Atlantic Express* and *Pacific Express* provided transcontinental service, with Chicago serving as the gateway to the eastern United States, San Francisco, and ultimately Asia.

However, the ordinary trains of the era cannot compare to the exclusive *Golden Gate Special* that debuted between Council Bluffs and the Bay Area in December 1888. In his book *Overland Limited*, Lucius Beebe, a writer known for plush prose and lush description said, "The Pullmans of the *Golden Gate Special* were a microcosm of luxury and convenience functioning in an almost lifeless void of plains and desert, sky and mountains, where fuel for the locomotives and water for the cars were almost the only resources of operation stops."

Intended to please the highest class of transcontinental traveler, the *Golden Gate Special* was dubbed "The Finest Train in the World." It comprised one set of palace cars—the fanciest, most ornate sleepers on American rails—and made just one roundtrip a week. Despite its overt opulence, the train failed commercially—service lasted less than one year. By 1889, the

Long-distance trains were themselves an advertising vehicle. By promoting the *San Francisco Overland Limited*, SP highlighted the superior infrastructure of its Overland Route. Here, SP boasted about its infrastructure and the railroad's ability to move both passenger and freight trains. *Author collection*

less opulent, yet still ornate, *Overland Flyer* (a train that had began running on Union Pacific in 1887) assumed the *Golden Gate Special*'s service. It wasn't until the late 1890s that the *Overland Limited*, as it was then known, was so identified in Central Pacific schedules.

This service variously operated as the *Overland Limited, San Francisco Overland Limited*, and *S.F. Overland Limited* (ritually known as simply the *Overland*) and was one the best-known trains in the West. In 1902, this premier run became one of the first trains to use steel-framed cars—significantly safer and more durable than the all-wooden passenger cars that predominated in nineteenth-century railroading. It carried an open observation car, and was equipped with the latest communication innovation: the telephone, which was connected only at the terminals.

In the mid-1920s, the *Overland* was running on a 58-hour schedule between Chicago and San Francisco—particularly impressive considering the Overland Route was not a contiguous all-rail line. Southern Pacific employed large steam-powered

Electro-Motive E2, diesels with insignia for Union Pacific, Chicago & North Western, and Southern Pacific indicating joint ownership of the equipment, on the first 102, the *City of San Francisco*. This is the second-generation streamliner from 1938, which replaced the original articulated lightweight train of 1936. Electro-Motive took its styling queues from parent General Motors. Note the overhead electric wires—at this time SP's suburban electrics were still in operation. *Fred Matthews collection*

ferries to move whole trains between Port Costa and Benicia, across Suisun Bay, until 1930 when the massive Carquinez Straits Bridge—the largest double-track railroad bridge west of the Mississippi River—was completed.

Gregory Thompson explains that in 1926, Southern Pacific invested in eight new train sets to overhaul the *Overland*. For a few years following World War II, the *Overland* was truly a transcontinental service, as it carried through sleepers for both New York City and Washington, D.C.

The westward *City of San Francisco* negotiates light snow at Truckee, California, in 1961. As the train gains elevation with its ascent of Donner, snowfall will become heavier and more intense. Most trips over the mountain were uneventful, as SP crews diligently worked to keep the line open. However, in January 1952, the westward *City* bogged down on the west slope at Yuba Pass, stranding passengers and making national news. *Bob Morris*

City of San Francisco

The streamlined era for American railroads blossomed in 1934, when Union Pacific debuted its three-unit *Streamliner* built by Pullman and powered by a Winton engine. Burlington's famous *Zephyr* hit the scene two months after *Streamliner*; together these trains demonstrated vastly improved rail-passenger transport. The *Streamliner*'s compact articulated, armor-yellow consist toured America to win the heart of the traveling public. Union Pacific had introduced a whole fleet of articulated, semi-permanently coupled, internal combustion–powered streamliners within a couple of years of the *Streamliner*'s debut.

These early trains with short fixed consists and built-in power cars proved impractical. Semi-permanently coupled train sets were inflexible and incapable of handling traffic growth. Union Pacific adopted trains that used conventionally coupled streamlined passenger cars, hauled either by new streamlined diesel-electric locomotives or streamlined steam locomotives. These were heavier but significantly more practical.

Union Pacific led its Overland Route partners Southern Pacific and Chicago & North Western to share the costs of the deluxe *City of San Francisco* streamliner, which began operation in 1936 on the traditional routing of the *Overland Limited*.

Unique to SP was the one former *City of San Francisco* E2A unit that, after 1947, was numbered 6011A and painted in the *Daylight* livery. Known as the "Queen Mary" in *Daylight* paint, it was no longer exclusive to the *City*, although it was still occasionally assigned to this service, as seen here in Oakland in March 1949. *Fred Matthews*

A quartet of Alco PAs lead the eastward *City of San Francisco* in 1961 across the 1930-built Suisun Bay Bridge. Completion of this massive double-track structure eliminated the need for the Carquinez Straits car ferries and significantly reduced travel time between Oakland and Sacramento. Today the Interstate 680 bridge parallels the old SP structure. *Bob Morris*

City of San Francisco was the first regularly scheduled diesel-powered passenger train to operate over SP. Initially, one train set, which measured 725 feet long and was powered by a pair of Winton 201A 1,200-horsepower engines, completed a single roundtrip every six days. Southern Pacific stressed the train's virtues in its advertising: "The new streamliner *City of San Francisco*. One day en route! 39 3/4 hours Chicago to San Francisco! Over the shortest route between San Francisco and Chicago now flashes an entirely new kind of train, *cutting a full day from regular schedules.*"

Comfort and speed were just two of the themes of the train:

Every new idea in comfortable, high speed travel has been built into the *City of San Francisco.* Its four Pullmans are of entirely new design. Many sections have sliding panels for complete privacy day and night. The upper berths have windows. A room car offers bedrooms for the first time between San Francisco and Chicago. There is a beautiful diner-lounge with a built-in radio. There is a de luxe chair car and coach-buffet car serving special low-priced meals for coach passengers. Both of these cars have radios, too.

112

Alco PAs lead train 102, the eastward *City of San Francisco,* over the original wooden trestle that crossed the Great Salt Lake. The *City* was operating daily by 1947. In 1959, SP opened a massive fill across the lake, replacing the 1903 trestle. *Southern Pacific photo, Bob Morris collection*

The *City of San Francisco* was an anomaly in SP's operations. The combination of its diesel engines and articulated passenger cars required specialized attention and facilities in Oakland, California. In the September 11, 1937, *Railway Age,* Southern Pacific's engineer of car construction, E. B. Dailey (who was also closely involved with the planning of the *Daylight*), provided a detailed account of SP's servicing of the original *City of San Francisco*:

With the introduction of the streamliner *City of San Francisco,* we realized that we would be confronted with a number of maintenance problems which would be new to us. This was due in a large part to the fact that this train is a complete unit, the nine cars all being articulated, which of course, means that they must be handled as a unit and cannot be separated.

Unlike the conventional steam train, which on arrival at the terminal, has the locomotive cut off and sent to the roundhouse, and the cars sent to the coach yard for cleaning and servicing, the streamliner power units and cars must be cleaned, serviced and repaired at one shop.

Dailey goes on to detail the turnaround of the train based on the rigorous six-day roundtrip schedule: "It arrives at 7:22 a.m. and departs at 4:08 p.m. the following day. It usually arrives at West Alameda shops at 9:00 a.m. and leaves the shop at 2:00 p.m. the following day. During this short stay all the work of inspecting and repairing must be done."

What seems remarkable today, in a world where diesels are the norm and are expected to run for tens of thousands of miles in hard service without incurring any serious repairs, is how much work was required to keep these primitive diesel-electrics running. At the time, they were making a 4,310-mile roundtrip weekly between Chicago and San Francisco. Dailey explains that it was routine procedure to change out three pistons on each trip and "to insure all pistons being replaced every 50,000 miles." Furthermore, "Cylinder heads are of course removed on the same schedule, re-conditioned by cleaning carbon and grinding valves, and later replaced." It is little wonder why, with this kind of intensive servicing, Southern Pacific officials were content to use modern steam locomotives on the new *Daylight*s.

Garmany notes in *Southern Pacific Dieselization* that the *City* could not maintain the published schedule without a steam helper over Donner Pass. A 4-6-0 was maintained at Roseville for the purpose of assisting the *City of San Francisco* over Donner east of Colfax to Norden.

A single heavyweight coach is the only passenger accommodation on the *Fast Mail*, seen here at Sparks, Nevada. Paying passengers were encouraged to ride fancy name trains instead of this all-stops long-distance local train. *Bob Morris*

Difficulties with the articulated lightweight train set and the general popularity of the *City of San Francisco* dictated ordering a new train of a better design and with more capacity. A new longer *City* consist entered service in January 1938 and a second train was assigned to the service in 1941 to allow two roundtrips a week. These trains used conventionally coupled streamlined cars to get away from the difficulties associated with articulated train sets. They were powered by early Electro-Motive E units that featured more opulent styling than the later E units. Daily service began in 1947, by which time the train was already operating triweekly. By the early 1950s, SP was routinely assigning Alco PAs in the *Daylight* livery to this run.

Sadly, the *City of San Francisco* is probably best remembered for two spectacular incidents that thrust it onto the front pages of newspapers everywhere. The first occurred on August 12, 1939, when train 101, the westward *City of San Francisco*, was racing toward the coast through Palisade Canyon, Nevada. Saboteurs had set a trap for the glorious train, diabolically and expertly disturbing the rails on an elevated curve while insuring the simple automatic block signaling would not reveal the damage. When the train came around the curve at an estimated speed of 60 miles per hour, a piece of sage had disguised the deliberate damage to the tracks. Within seconds the

Although carried in the timetable, in later years passengers were not encouraged to ride trains 21 and 22, which was primarily operated for mail and express traffic. Train 21, *Fast Mail*, pauses for its long station stop at Reno, Nevada. An FP7A leads four Alco PA/PBs. The train's slow schedule and numerous stops were for mail delivery, not passenger comfort. *Bob Morris*

train derailed and careened out of control and several cars were dumped into the Humboldt River. The disaster killed 25 people. Southern Pacific Vice President J. H. Dyer, President Angus McDonald, and other officials raced to the scene of the crash to aid rescue efforts. The wrecking of the *City of San Francisco* was big news, although it would soon be eclipsed by dramatic events on the German-Polish border. Although SP, the ICC, and the FBI conducted a thorough investigation at the scene, the perpetrators were never caught.

The second event occurred on Sunday, January 13, 1952. A fierce blizzard raged on Donner and SP had dispatched its massive Leslie rotary plows to clear the tracks. Train 101, the westward *City of San Francisco*, led by three *Daylight*-painted PA/PBs, was held inside the sheds at Norden, but was allowed to proceed when it was deemed safe. Descending Donner, it made it as far as Yuba Pass, where the streamliner encountered an impassible snow slide. The train bogged down and it was snowing so hard that in no time the train was snowbound. Initial efforts to free the *City* from the icy clutches of the Sierra failed and the train and its passengers were trapped for three days. When the heating eventually failed, the passengers survived the ordeal by keeping warm with blankets. At times the wind outside the train was estimated at as high as 80 miles per hour, making efforts to shovel the train free fruitless. While no one aboard No. 101 was killed during the incident, the engineer of a rotary plow trying to reach the stalled train died when his plow train derailed. Newspapers featured the stalled train for several days until the passengers were finally freed and brought to safety on January 16, 1952.

The Sunset Route logo was one of SP's oldest and best-known insignia. It is seen here on an ornamental plate carried by restored Electro-Motive E9 6051. The setting sun over steel rails is a romantic vision of the SP that outlasted the company's passenger service and was used on railroad literature until SP's 1997 inclusion in Union Pacific. *Brian Solomon*

Other Overland Trains

The *City* streamliners were just one step in a large-scale overhaul of transcontinental services via the Overland Route. To augment the original *City of San Francisco*, the Overland railroads, on July 11, 1937, introduced the *Forty Niner*, a steam-powered, streamlined all-Pullman train that also operated about every six days. On May 22, 1940, the *Treasure Island Special* debuted as a summer schedule extra-fare service between Chicago and the Bay Area. According to the April 20, 1940, *Railway Age*, it carried a baggage car, six lightweight Pullman sleepers, a dining car, and a lounge observation. Its livery was light gray. It was short lived, however, and ceased operation after the 1940 summer season. The *Forty Niner* was discontinued in July 1941.

In autumn 1937, Union Pacific (UP), Chicago & North Western (C&NW), and SP introduced an air-conditioned economy overnight service called the *San Francisco Challenger*, patterned after Union Pacific's *Challenger*, which operated between Chicago and Los Angeles. According to the September 4, 1937, *Railway Age*, the *San Francisco Challenger* carried chair cars and tourist sleepers, as well as a lounge car and bar. To make the train more appealing the train featured a car exclusively for women and children travelers with a qualified stewardess/nurse. All three participating railroads helped purchase passenger cars for the train. The May 14, 1938, *Railway Age* reported that Southern Pacific's chair cars purchased for the service were almost identical to those bought for the *Daylight*.

Bridge over Salton Sea--S. P. R. R.
California--Arizona Route

Southern Pacific's Sunset Route crossed the Salton Sink in the southern California desert east of Indio. This depression is well below sea level, making the SP by far the lowest mainline in North America. Early in the twentieth century, agricultural interests detoured the Colorado River into the sink. Due to poor planning the water raged out of control, causing the depression to flood and ultimately resulting in the Salton Sea. As the floodwater rose over several years, SP was forced to relocate its mainline. A deluxe luxury limited, probably the *Sunset Limited* or *Golden State Limited*, poses on a trestle across the man-made lake. Note the arched windows on the side of the open-end observation car. *Author collection*

Often eclipsed by better-known luxury trains and fast streamliners were workhorse secondary runs like the *Pacific Limited* (trains 19/20) and Nos. 9 and 10, sometimes known as the *Fast Mail*.

Sunset Route

Perhaps the best-known symbolic representation of Southern Pacific is the famous insignia depicting glistening rails heading toward the resplendent globe of the setting sun. This neatly embodies the romance of the West and the progress of man. It is a visual representation of Horace Greeley's advice that encouraged generations of Americans to look westward. Southern Pacific historians Neill C. Wilson and Frank J. Taylor credit the origin of this famous insignia to a Texas & New Orleans employee named N. R. Olcott, who is said to have sketched it in 1876. Regardless of its origin, the railroad adapted the sunset logo in dozens of ways over the years, and it was often featured on company documents and equipment. It is difficult to say precisely when SP officially adopted the Sunset Route name, but by 1892—two years prior to the introduction of its namesake limited —the Sunset Route was being advertised in promotional literature.

The Sunset Route connected the Pacific Coast and the Gulf of Mexico, running from Los Angeles to New Orleans. SP, having reached Los Angeles by September 1876, kept pushing eastward, following the surveys of William Hood. By 1877, it had reached the Colorado River at Yuma, Arizona, and by May 19, 1881, rails had connected El Paso, Texas. SP's through route to New Orleans was completed with connection to its Texas lines on January 12, 1883. In order to comply with legal requirements that lines in Texas be operated locally, SP maintained Texas subsidiaries and after 1927, SP routes in Texas and Louisiana were operated under the umbrella of its Texas & New Orleans subsidiary.

Continued on page 123

117

New Orleans —
one of America's three "story cities"

And then, on to California!

MARDI GRAS,
*the renowned New Orleans Mid-
winter Carnival, January
7th to February 12th*

WHICH are the three most interesting cities in America? Frank Norris, famous novelist, declared them to be New York, New Orleans and San Francisco. "Story cities", he called them.

Southern Pacific, by steamship and rail, presents all three of these fascinating cities to the traveler in a single journey. You can take comfortable Southern Pacific steamship at New York, enjoy "100 golden hours at sea" en route to California, and debark at New Orleans for a pleasurable stopover in the city that has lived under five flags.

You will turn irresistibly to the old French Quarter, every building of which is haunted with memories and legends. You will pass the site where stood the slave block in days before the Civil War. And you will turn with delight to the Mississippi River levees.

Here is quaintest Dixie! The modern, throbbing, vital city of New Orleans can never lose its foreign flavor.

And then, continuing your journey on "*Sunset Limited*" or "*The Argonaut*", you will be carried swiftly and smoothly across Louisiana, Texas and the Spanish-American Southwest.

Travelers to the Pacific Coast via the Sunset Route may also start their journey from other points than New York, taking the most convenient rail lines to New Orleans. Return journey from California can be any one of *four* Southern Pacific routes. Stopovers may be taken anywhere. This affords opportunity to see the whole Pacific Coast.

· · · · ·

Your name and address to E. W. CLAPP, traffic manager, Dept. C-26, 310 S. Michigan Blvd., Chicago, will bring you without charge a highly interesting book with illustrations and animated maps, "*How Best to See the Pacific Coast*", and a handsome brochure, "*New Orleans, the Crescent City*".

Southern Pacific
Four Great Routes

SUNSET ROUTE—"*Sunset Limited*"
GOLDEN STATE ROUTE—"*Golden State Limited*"
OVERLAND ROUTE—"*San Francisco Overland Limited*"
SHASTA ROUTE—"*The Cascade*"

This 1929 advertisement for Southern Pacific's Sunset Route cites novelist Frank Norris—ironic considering his best-known work, *The Octopus*, had essentially vilified SP. *Author collection*

On SP's Texas & New Orleans (T&NO) subsidiary Dallas–Houston overnight run, trains 17 and 18 were known as the *Owl* but should not be confused with the Oakland–Los Angeles trains of the same name. On July 27, 1936, T&NO P-6 Pacific 621 built by Alco-Brooks in 1913 leads train 18 with 10 cars at Houston. In 1943, the T&NO *Owl* was allowed 7 1/2 hours between Dallas and Houston. *Otto Perry, Denver Public Library Western History Collection*

Southern Pacific's line through the Carriso Gorge via the San Diego & Arizona Eastern has achieved almost mythic status. This route connected El Centro and San Diego, California, crossing the border with Mexico several times. The line's engineering was especially impressive, passing through numerous rocky tunnels and over tall wooden trestles. In this vintage postcard, an SP 4-6-0, likely a Class T-31, leads a tidy passenger train of heavyweight cars, possibly the San Diego section of the *Argonaut. Author collection*

In 1951, Southern Pacific used this advertisement for the new streamlined *Sunset Limited* to stress its enormous postwar investment in new equipment. Southern cotton farmers wave to gleaming Alco PAs with "1" in the numberboards. The *Sunset Limited* was one of America's finest trains. *Author collection*

Railroad advertising in the 1920s promoted travel and a general sense of wonder. Here, SP's *Sunset Limited* offers views of the old Missions along the route. SP promoted both its most deluxe train and its secondary counterpart, the *Argonaut*, which operated a section via Carriso Gorge to San Diego. *Author collection*

The *Imperial* offered an alternate routing between Chicago and Los Angeles through the Imperial Valley of Southern California. The Sunset Route was not just a single set of tracks, but an east–west corridor consisting of several different lines offering alternate routings. *Author collection*

SP's very last new streamlined car, No. 150, the *Sunset*, built by Pullman in 1955, is an unusual example of an open-platform streamlined observation car. Most streamlined observation cars had enclosed rounded or squared-off ends. This luxurious business car was entirely self-contained, complete with generators to provide electricity for all onboard needs. It is seen on the back of a business train climbing Cuesta in March 1993. *Brian Solomon*

IT'S HERE!... Another fast train between CHICAGO and LOS ANGELES

THE IMPERIAL

THE INTERNATIONAL LIMITED

VIA SOUTHERN ARIZONA-OLD MEXICO-IMPERIAL VALLEY

FAST! This new train streaks from Chicago to Los Angeles over the Golden State Route (Rock Island-Southern Pacific) daily in just 53 hours, makes the return trip, eastbound, in 52¼ hours. Although faster than pre-war trains over this route, there is no extra fare on the *Imperial*.

CONVENIENT! The *Imperial* leaves Chicago at 11:00 a.m., daily, arrives Los Angeles 2:00 p.m., second day following. Eastbound, this new train leaves Los Angeles at 11:00 a.m., arrives in Chicago at 5:15 p.m.

COMFORTABLE! Standard sleeping cars on the *Imperial* provide both private room and section space. In addition, the *Imperial* carries a standard Pullman between Kansas City and Los Angeles as well as special sleeping cars for both Tucson and Phoenix. Modern chair cars and coaches are also carried on the

Imperial, and a comfortable, roomy lounge car is provided for Pullman passengers. The immaculate dining car serves delicious full meals to all.

INTERNATIONAL AND SCENIC! the *Imperial* gives you an exciting 51-mile trip through Old Mexico, and shows you California's sunny Imperial Valley.

5 FINE, FAST TRAINS DAILY TO THE SOUTHWEST SUN COUNTRY

The *Sunset Limited* and *Argonaut* on the Sunset Route from New Orleans and the *Golden State Limited*, *Californian* and the new *Imperial* on the Golden State Route from Chicago, provide the fastest daily main line trains direct to El Paso, Tucson, Phoenix, and other resort and guest ranch centers in the southwest.

A-61 (10-28-46) 135M—Standard Folder—Form A—November 10, 1946—Subject to change without notice—Printed in U.S.A.

Southern Pacific's Texas & New Orleans affiliate ran the *Arcadian* (trains 3/4) on the Sunset Route train between New Orleans and Houston. This 1936 view at Houston portrays T&NO P-5 Pacific 607 leading a six-car train with a railway post office, baggage car, and four heavyweight passenger cars. The *Arcadian* typically carried standard Pullman sleeping cars offering passengers a selection of section berths, drawing rooms, and compartments. In addition, it also carried coaches and, in later years, chair cars. *Otto Perry, Denver Public Library Western History Department*

As Los Angeles grew in importance, so did SP's Sunset Route. By the late twentieth century, the Sunset was among the heaviest-traveled freight lines in the West. However, the line remains best known for its namesake train, the *Sunset Limited*. Lucius Beebe, again waxing eloquently about America's luxury limiteds, wrote of the *Sunset Limited* in his book *The Overland Limited*:

> The New York Central's *Twentieth Century Limited* can legitimately lay claim to greater world renown and status as an American institution. The level of voluptuousness was immeasurably more exalted on the Santa Fe's most exquisitely appointed *De Luxe* and upon the Southern Pacific's ranking candy train of all time, *The Sunset Limited* in its finest flowering at the turn of the century.

Eventually, Beebe finds words to relate on the subject of his book, but dwells to relay an interesting 1905 episode regarding the *Sunset Limited*, whether real, embellished, or a figment of imagination, crediting a manifestation of the Old West in this event: "When, at Phoenix, Arizona, an English dude was lassoed from the Observation platform of the *Sunset Limited* for staring at the peasantry through a single eyeglass."

The first regular through passenger services on the Sunset Route were operated with a pair of trains known as the *Pacific Express* westward and *Atlantic Express* eastward. According to John Signor in his book *Tehachapi*, these trains were sometimes collectively known as *The Sunset Express*.

In its original incarnation, beginning in Autumn 1894, the *Sunset Limited* was an exclusive, extra-fare service operating once per week between San Francisco and New Orleans by way of the Central Valley, the Tehachapis, and Los Angeles. At that time Los Angeles was a mere town in comparison with the established California metropolis of San Francisco, the latter, of course, being the logical and desirable destination for all right-thinking travelers.

Arthur Dubin, in *Some Classic Trains*, tells that SP's early *Sunset Limited* advertisements appealed to travelers wishing to avoid the perils of traveling over the mountains, especially in winter. To attract transcontinental traffic, SP offered connecting steamship service between New Orleans and New York City on a five-day schedule. Dubin also explains that, in the early years of the twentieth century, *Sunset Limited* frequency varied from once a week to three times per week. Interestingly, the train was suspended after 1904 and didn't resume operation until 1911, two years after Harriman's death. Then, at end of 1913, the train assumed a daily schedule.

Sunset Streamliners

In the late 1930s, when new diesel streamliners were the rage on American railways, Southern Pacific seriously considered operating the ultimate American streamlined

The *Sunset Limited* had long been Southern Pacific's finest train, and in 1950 it was entirely retrofitted using five completely new sets of streamlined equipment. By the early 1960s, when this photo was made, the train was running with a mix of cars from SP's long-distance passenger pool. *Southern Pacific photo, John Signor collection*

Prior to the debut of the new Budd-built streamliner *Sunset Limited*, SP posed a portion of the classy new train for publicity photos. The train operated with two or more E units and a full consist of passenger cars. Locomotive 6018 was built in 1949 and was the railroad's sole E8. The inaugural consist of *Sunset Limited* had 15 cars, including a baggage-mail railway post office (pictured), a baggage-crew dorm, four chair cars, a coffee-shop lounge car, six sleeping cars, a dining car, and a buffet-lounge car. *Southern Pacific photo, Bob Morris collection*

train, a Washington, D.C.–to–Los Angeles deluxe diesel limited to be named *Robert E. Lee*. Had it run, it would have been operated in conjunction with the Louisville & Nashville and Southern Railway to hold a tight 59-hour coast-to-coast schedule. Although an exciting prospect, SP shelved the plan.

In 1946 and 1947, SP announced plans to revamp its grand dame of luxury limiteds, the old *Sunset Limited*, which after years of relative neglect during the Great Depression and hard work during the crush of World War II, was in desperate need of a makeover. Southern Pacific tendered bids for no less than five complete streamlined train sets. But, as in the case with its other postwar streamliners, the train was delayed in production and finally made ready in 1950. Unlike the majority of SP's streamlined trains which used Pullman-built lightweight cars, the *Sunset Limited* stood out because the railroad ordered cars from the Philadelphia-based Budd Company. In 1947 dollars, the estimated cost for the five trains, including diesel-electric locomotives, was placed at $15 million, making this SP's largest, but also its last, major investment in a new long-distance passenger train.

On August 20, 1950, just one week after launching its new streamlined *Cascade*, SP debuted its magnificent new *Sunset Limited*. To make the most of its investment, SP coordinated an intensive media blitz to promote its flagship train. John Garmany called the *Sunset Limited* the "ultimate expression of luxury travel" and went on to explain that SP had neither spared expense nor glossed over detail in making the *Sunset Limited* the finest train on the railroad. John Harbeson, who incorporated regional and historic themes from along the line, designed the interior décor. One car displayed the aura of New Orleans' French Quarter and featured wrought-iron grillwork and a brilliant watermelon-red ceiling. According to Garmany, this color inspired "Sunset Pink," which was promoted in fashion circles that year. The dining cars featured drawings by famous naturalist John James Audubon, and the train operated on a much-accelerated schedule, making the 2,070-mile run in just 42 hours.

Although the *Sunset* gets all the glory, it was one of only several name trains on the route. For many years the second-best Sunset Route passenger train was the *Argonaut*, allusively named after the golden fleece seekers of Greek myth. This train took a different routing across Arizona, diverging from the mainline and using the main freight line across central Arizona, skipping Phoenix.

Sunbeam and *Hustler*

Outside of California, one of SP's most significant long-distance intrastate routes was the 265-mile Dallas–Houston corridor. According to Don Hofsommer, in 1930 this line boasted three name trains daily—*Sunbeam*, *Hustler*, an overnight sleeper called

Houston-to-Dallas *Sunbeam* streamliner appeared as a foreshortened *Daylight*. SP rebuilt three Class P-6 Pacifics in 1937 specifically for this service, which were reclassified as P-14s. In addition to functional changes, such as the use of Boxpok drivers, the locomotives featured modern streamlined styling in a manner consistent with all-new Lima-built GS-2 4-8-4s. *J. R. Quinn collection*

This 1945 SP timetable features a stylized P-14 Pacific normally assigned to the *Sunbeam*. Wartime austerity resulted in printing timetables on cheap paper. Thick, glossy-covered timetables returned after restrictions were eased. *Author collection*

This World War II–era Shasta timetable illustrates SP's most modern equipment, including the 1938 *City of San Francisco* diesel streamliner. *Author collection*

the *Owl* (not to be confused with the Oakland–Los Angeles train of the same name)—plus a typical all-stops local. Politically, this was an important region for SP, and shortly after the *Daylight* made its splashy debut on the Coast Line, Southern Pacific introduced a comparable service on the Dallas–Houston run by upgrading the *Sunbeam* (trains 13/14) with a pair of streamlined trains. These eight-car streamliners used lightweight Pullman-built cars with corrugated-steel sheathing similar to those on the *Daylight*. They were hauled by 4-6-2 Pacific-type steam locomotives that had been rebuilt with *Daylight*-style streamlined shrouding, rather than brand-new streamlined 4-8-4s. The trains were painted in the *Daylight* livery and consisted of a baggage car, four two-piece articulated coaches (like those used on the *Daylight*), a nonarticulated coach, a parlor car, and a round-end observation car containing dining and lounge facilities. As built, the train carried 228 passenger seats, about half of the *Daylight*. Streamlined service began on September 19, 1937. This train was very popular with riders and management, and was augmented in 1938 with the introduction of the streamlined *Hustler* (trains 14/15). The Texas streamliners looked like mini-*Daylight*s.

Golden State Route

Of the dozen or so North American transcontinental routes, one of the least remarked-upon is the Golden State Route. Completed relatively late, this route has a relatively low-altitude crossing of the Continental Divide and thus doesn't feature the spectacular scenery or wondrous engineering that characterized many of the better-known transcontinental lines. In 1902, Chicago, Rock Island & Pacific connected a line then known as the El Paso & Rock Island at Santa Rosa, New Mexico. (The latter railroad was later part of the El Paso & Southwestern [EP&SW], which was controlled by Arizona's Phelps Dodge copper interests. This route briefly threatened to rival

Newer steam power was assigned to the *Daylight* and other name trains when Otto Perry exposed this photo of the first streamlined *Daylight* locomotive, GS-2 No. 4410, leading train 47 with 10 cars. This train primarily carried mail and express over the Golden State Route, and is seen here crossing the desert near Coyote, New Mexico, on September 22, 1947. *Otto Perry, Denver Public Library Western History Department*

Southern Pacific's Sunset Route and may have presented serious competition had it ever reached Los Angeles.) This route connected with Southern Pacific at El Paso, forming a through chord, Chicago to Los Angeles. Shortly after it opened, the Golden State hosted a new posh luxury limited appropriately named the *Golden State Limited*.

The Golden State Route became a more important part of SP's western empire in the 1920s. In 1924, SP acquired the EP&SW, cementing its Golden State Route connections while expanding capacity on the Sunset Route between Tucson and El Paso, and eliminating the potential of direct competition for California traffic from Rock Island/ EP&SW.

Despite this move, the Golden State Route never enjoyed the status of either the Overland or Sunset Routes, and remained something of a second-tier freight route. As evidence of its lesser status, the line never received major upgrading and was characterized by basic lower-quadrant block signals and single-track desert running with short passing sidings. Weak-sister status was further reflected in SP's attitudes toward its postwar Golden State Route passenger services.

After World War II, Rock Island was anxious to introduce a luxury streamliner that would compete with Santa Fe's hot *Super Chief*. Rock Island urged SP to create the *Golden Rocket* along the lines of Rock Island's own *Rocket* family of trains. Southern

The streamlined *Golden State* was Southern Pacific's compromise with Rock Island to replace the planned *Golden Rocket*. Both SP and Rock Island contributed equipment to the *Golden State* and this round-end Pullman observation car was a Rock Island car. It featured large rear windows, making it a relatively unusual streamlined car. *Southern Pacific photo, John Signor collection*

Interior view of the diner on the jointly run Rock Island/Southern Pacific streamlined *Golden State,* which operated from Chicago to Los Angeles via Tucumcari, New Mexico, and El Paso, Texas. *Richard Jay Solomon collection*

Pacific tentatively agreed, but to match Santa Fe, the Golden State Route needed an upgrade, as the railroad was formulating its plans for each of its historic Four Scenic Routes. Yet, enthusiasm for the *Golden Rocket* was all on Rock Island's shoulders. To equip the *Golden Rocket,* Rock Island placed an order with Pullman. According to Garmany, these cars featured beautifully designed interior décor by Ralph Haman, Pullman's "Engineer of Color and Design," who used Mexican themes that would resonate with travelers as they passed near the Mexican border. Despite some early advertising for the *Golden Rocket* and big plans for a Hollywood-style media storm by the Rock, Southern Pacific decided not to participate after all, scuttling the train. Instead, SP upgraded the *Golden State Limited* with new streamlined equipment, along with a streamlined name—"*Limited*" was dropped with the introduction of new equipment. A short item in the December 13, 1947, *Railway Age* offered this announcement:

"The *Golden State,* diesel-powered streamliner operated by the Chicago, Rock Island & Pacific and the Southern Pacific between Chicago and Los Angeles, Cal.,

The late Roger Puta at El Paso, Texas, photographed Southern Pacific's lone E8A, No. 6018 in the 1958 scarlet and gray livery after hauling the westward *Golden State* on March 25, 1967. After 1965, the *Sunset* and *Golden State* were routinely combined west of El Paso. *Roger Puta, Brian Jennison collection*

will be placed on a high-speed, extra-fare schedule beginning on January 4, 1948. Coincident with the inauguration of the new schedule will be the addition to the train of new lightweight cars sheathed with stainless steel."

Railway Age made no mention of the much faster schedule the Rock hoped to assign the *Golden Rocket*, but gave this explanation to its readers, who by then were anticipating the *Golden Rocket*'s debut:

"Because of unavoidable delays in receiving sufficient equipment necessary to operate the Chicago–Los Angeles *Golden Rocket*—which the Rock Island and Southern Pacific had planned to inaugurate this month—the roads are assigning to the *Golden State* the equipment which has been received for use on the new trains."

Southern Pacific management had a variety of issues with the *Golden Rocket* that precluded it from making the investment. Fred Matthews relates that Rock Island's hopes for an extra-fast schedule to match Santa Fe's would have required substantial upgrading of tracks and signals, an investment SP was unwilling to make. At this time the ICC was preparing new regulations on the operation of high-speed trains following a disastrous crash on the Burlington in 1946. Another consideration was an underlying purpose for such a luxury limited, which was to promote the status of the Golden State Route as a premier freight corridor, which obviously SP believed only justified the level of investment and promotion for a second-tier corridor. In truth, the upgraded *Golden State* was SP's compromise with Rock Island to improve service.

Among the secondary trains on the Golden State Route was the economy-minded *Californian* (trains 43/44), operating Los Angeles to Chicago, which carried chair cars, coaches, tourist sleepers, and standard section sleepers. The *Imperial* operated on the Golden State Route and was so named because it deviated from the main stem of the Sunset Route at Niland to serve the Imperial Valley and El Centro. In later days, this was effectively just a mail and express run carrying a few chair cars to accommodate passengers.

SP once had extensive operations south of the border. Its timetables for the West Coast of Mexico typically occupied the rear pages of its public timetable. By the mid-1940s, services were limited to a triweekly overnight train, *El Costene*, and a triweekly mixed service that also carried Pullman sleepers. These provided service between Nogales and Guadalajara, and to Mexico City via the National Railways of Mexico. There were also connections from Nogales to Los Angeles. In addition, SP's Mexican branchlines still ran a variety of mixed services. *Author collection*

Demise and the Coming of Amtrack

By the time of this 1964 view of the *Shasta Daylight*—seen rounding the Cantara Loop near Dunsmuir, California—the train was operating a foreshortened consist on just a triweekly schedule. Once considered one of SP's finest streamlined trains, it was discontinued altogether in 1966, leaving the overnight *Cascade* as the line's premier passenger train. Today this is the route of Amtrak's *Coast Starlight*. *Bob Morris*

S outhern Pacific's passenger trains were its public face. Its trains provided a public service, and for many years they provided very good service. To maintain this service, the company made an enormous investment in equipment, passenger stations, advertising, and operations. So what changed? What went wrong? When did Southern Pacific's passenger operations run into trouble? And why did Southern Pacific ultimately abandon its passenger trains?

SP's passenger train problems roughly mirrored problems faced by railroads throughout America. Yet, SP's latter-day reaction to its problems set it apart from many other railroads. It was one of the first railroads to drastically scale back its long-distance network, which, as Fred Matthews illustrates in Chapter 1, gave it a harsh reputation as being anti-passenger.

Roots of Decline

Passenger train problems were not suddenly thrust on the railroads. Southern Pacific accountants did not wake up one morning to find

133

that the company's trains were, without warning, losing millions of dollars. Difficulties came on slowly and for the most part were well known to railroad managers. As early as the 1890s, railroad moguls like James J. Hill had declared that passenger trains were money losers. To the public it might seem that SP ran into difficulties after World War II and reacted negatively when passenger operations suddenly ran in the red. In reality, the situation went back long before the war.

Gregory Lee Thompson in *The Passenger Train in the Motor Age* offers a very detailed account of the decline of the passenger train in California with a focus on Southern Pacific. Understanding what happened in California gives us a picture of what occurred to passenger operations across the United States. Since California was the focus of SP's most intensive passenger operations, this analysis allows a special insight into SP problems and why they occurred.

Thompson suggests that the seeds of the SP passenger decline in California were sown very early in the railroad's tenure and that the passenger train's influence in California peaked around 1910. Among the underlying causes for the erosion of Southern Pacific's transportation supremacy was SP's loss of political clout in the years prior to World War I. The railroad's goals were at odds with California's business interests, and SP suffered from a backlash because of its perceived transportation monopoly and unwillingness to provide the level of transport desired by business. The public reaction was the construction of competitive public infrastructure and the rise of motor transport. This occurred as SP's public influence was on the wane. California was one of the first states to make enormous public investment in highways, but Thompson explains that this large-scale public investment was just part of the problem. He argues that SP management did not react appropriately or early enough to stem the tide of highway competition. Traditional railroad business practices and a fundamental misunderstanding of SP's cost structures by its management led them to mis-assess the market and make decisions that ultimately undermined the company's ability to run passenger trains profitably. Thompson writes:

An SP Atlantic with very tall drivers marches out of San Jose with wooden heavyweight cars around 1910. This was the golden age of SP passenger services in the days before government-funded highways subsidized motor transport competition. At the time, SP had a virtual monopoly on most transport in California and throughout the Southwest. *Richard Jay Solomon collection*

3510 The Southern Pacific Broad Gauge Depot, San Jose, California.

The allure of a T-31 Ten-Wheeler and four heavyweight cars couldn't compare with the freedom offered by the automobile. Train 4, the San Diego section of the *Golden State Limited*, departs San Diego, California, on April 23, 1933. It will operate via Mexico, the famous Carriso Gorge, and El Centro, California. According to Guy Dunscomb, 2353 was regularly assigned to SP's San Diego & Arizona Eastern affiliate. *Otto Perry, Denver Public Library Western History Department*

Rather than viewing passenger service as a significant source of profit, railroad managers saw it as a means of gaining competitive advantage over other railroads in the pursuit of freight traffic. This view led them to ignore important public preferences through the 1920s. In the early 1930s, management showed greater market sensitivity, but profitability eluded them because of their ignorance of the cost consequences of their passenger decisions.

By the 1930s, quality highways in California gave automotive transport a decided edge over SP's passenger trains. Automobile travel often got you to your destination faster and with greater freedom and flexibility than could SP's trains. SP's reaction was mixed. In the early 1920s, trhe railroad continued to offer a wide range of rural and local passenger train services despite intensifying competition from highway transport. Finally, in the late 1920s, SP refocused its services, converting some rural local operations to buses, completely abandoning several local passenger hubs, and putting greater emphasis on long-distance runs that were less susceptible to highway competition.

On a national scale, a fundamental problem facing most railroads was the inequitable situation between transportation modes as a result of state and federal subsidy. In 1959, David P. Morgan summed this up in *TRAINS Magazine*, in an article titled "Who Shot the Passenger Train?":

Of all modes of transport in the U.S., the railroad (and hence the passenger train) is the only one excluding pipelines which provides and maintains its own physical plant out of private capital and is taxed as a property owner. Obviously the passenger, then, must be charged the full costs of the service plus, in theory at least, a reasonable return on the investment. Just as obviously competitive pricing is based upon tax-free public plant financed by Government monies. The net effect is to cancel out the superior technological economy of the passenger train as compared with its winged or rubberized rivals. . . . Summed up, the passenger train is a private plant pitted against a public plant

Yet, it is unlikely that railroad service could have continued at its World War I–era growth rates even if public policies and subsidies had not favored highways and, later, airlines. The railroads' real problems were *why* they were left out of public spending and *how* publicly sponsored transport created competition to privately funded transport, questions that are more difficult to decipher.

On a national level, railroad management was highly distrustful of government and potential intervention with their business. The brief period of government control of American railroads brought about by poor service during World War I acerbated railroad management's already negative opinion of government intervention. One result of short-lived government control was an unwillingness to ask for, or accept, government assistance for infrastructure improvements, or subsidies for unprofitable services. Related to this problem was the long-held public expectation that railroads had a *responsibility* to provide passenger service, even if this incurred operating losses; the

The Martinez, California, station in April 1950, was a busy place. Train 224, the eastward *Senator* heading for Sacramento, approaches its station stop. Meanwhile on the opposite track, head-end business is unloaded from late-running train 57, the *Owl* from Los Angeles. Today the railroad plays second fiddle to the constant parade of highway traffic crossing the Carquinez Straits on Interstate 680. *Fred Matthews*

136

Continued on page 140

On October 18 and 19, 1958, Southern Pacific operated the *Reno Express* from Oakland's 16th Street Station (with bus connection to the Ferry Building in San Francisco) to Reno, Nevada, over the Sierra. This was the final public farewell to steam power on SP, and GS-6 4460 did the honors. By 1958, most regular steam operations on SP had already concluded (steam commute services ended in January 1957). Steam operations continued on SP's Mexican affiliate, Nacazori Railway until January 1959. This locomotive has been preserved and is now a static display in St. Louis. *Fred Matthews*

Opposite top: Alco PAs arrive with the *Shasta Daylight* at the Oakland Pier about 1953. Among SP's late-1950s austerity moves was discontinuance of its Oakland–San Francisco ferries and closure of the Oakland Pier. After July 1958, most long-distance trains terminated at Oakland's 16th Street Station. *Fred Matthews*

Opposite bottom: The *City of San Francisco*'s PAs idle beneath the ancient sheds at the Oakland Pier on February 9, 1957. Passengers would disembark from the trains and board steam ferries for San Francisco. In later years, SP used bus connections. *Fred Matthews*

Above: SP's passenger services were in transition in the late 1950s. In a few years time this whole scene at the Oakland Mole will have changed. From left to right: a steam farewell special, *San Joaquin Daylight*, led by Electro-Motive F units in Black Widow paint; train 10, the *Shasta Daylight*, behind a pair of PAs; train 224, the *Senator*, bound for Sacramento with a single PA and a mix of heavyweight and lightweight cars; and, just sticking its nose out on the far right, a Fairbanks-Morse switcher. *Fred Matthews*

assumption was that passenger losses would be compensated by freight revenues. Thompson asserts that SP management believed maintaining passenger services was necessary to promote goodwill and to market freight services.

The concept of public funding seems to have been beyond the corporate culture of the times. Yet, in the late 1920s, if the railroads had been allocated public funds for infrastructure improvements and subsidies for publicly important, but deficit-generating, passenger services, many valuable services might have been retained. For example, SP's extensive electric operations in Los Angeles and the Bay Area were a drain on company resources, but provided a valuable public service.

SP's Ineffectual Responses to Competition

Despite dramatic escalation of publicly sponsored infrastructure improvements, SP was slow to make substantive changes in its passenger policy. Through the 1920s, although it began to place greater emphasis on long-distance trains, SP introduced its own bus services to cut costs, and scaled back local train services in reaction to erosion of local business by highway transport and SP's changing traffic patterns.

More interesting, as Thompson illustrates, were SP's bold reactions in the mid-1930s that were more a response to Santa Fe's plans to invade SP's territory than to specifically counter highway competition. Its consultants had suggested running low-cost, high-speed internal combustion trains on medium-distance, high-density corridors, specifically the Bay Area–Sacramento market. However, SP's conservative management took a reactive approach. Instead of lowering costs, SP went for an image makeover to counter Santa Fe's threat of competition. SP promoted its Coast Line and built sexy streamlined trains because that is what it feared Santa Fe was

As the sun pierces the morning fog at Martinez, California, Black Widow–painted Electro-Motive GP9 5892, leading the *Senator*, meets PAs on the *Cascade* arriving from Portland. Discontinued on May 31, 1962, trains 223/224, the *Senator*s, were the last Oakland–Sacramento locals. Compare this image with the photo on page 136 made a dozen years earlier. *Bob Morris*

Southern Pacific bought SDP45s to replace worn-out PAs and E units on passenger trains. These powerful, business-looking locomotives worked SP's name trains and commute services in the final years of passenger services. Sunset at Rodeo, California, finds the passing of the Oakland–Portland *Cascade*, led by 3204. *Bob Morris*

going to use. So SP chose a design that embodied new technology and styling, but did not offer the cost advantages of diesel-powered lightweight streamliners.

Southern Pacific believed that its fancy luxury streamliners would attract passengers while portraying the company in a positive light. In this respect, SP followed the consultants' advice by making trains more appealing while aggressively selling its services through shrewd marketing and competitive pricing.

SP embraced new lightweight passenger car technology that lowered tare weight, which, in theory, should have lowered the cost of operation. But according to Thompson, SP's application of lightweight train technology was misguided and had the effect of increasing its operating costs rather than reducing them. Despite this apparent flawed technological application, in the short term, SP's streamliners proved successful, attracting passengers back to the rails and carrying very heavy loads. Furthermore, by the railroad's own cost analysis, these trains operated at a profit. Thompson, however, disagrees with the way railroads calculated their costs, explaining that despite apparent success, the higher cost of operating streamliners may have in fact weakened the financial viability of long-distance services. By this logic, SP would have either needed to lower the cost of running streamliners while retaining high ridership, or alternatively, find a way to attract equal or greater numbers using traditional heavyweight trains.

As it happened, the latter scenario occurred by accident due to World War II. For a few years, SP, and virtually all American railroads, were carrying record volumes

of passengers. Gasoline rationing, government restrictions, and increased economic activity, combined with the enormous need to transport military personnel, pushed American railroads to the limits of their passenger-carrying capacities. SP was in an especially good position to move record numbers of people. As its October 14, 1943, public timetable pointed out:

> Southern Pacific serves more military and naval establishments than any other railroad in the U.S. From New Orleans to Portland an endless chair of air bases and encampments adjoins our line.
>
> We serve more military meals to personnel of the armed forces than any other *two* U.S. railroads combined.

Budd RDC 10 was involved in an accident and SP rebuilt it as a single-ended car, making it an unusual machine. In 1962, it is seen running toward Eureka, California, along Scotia Bluffs on the NWP. *Bob Morris*

142

Budd built a single rail diesel car (RDC) for Southern Pacific in 1953. Originally, this was assigned to work Oakland–Sacramento local services as encouraged by the California Public Utilities Commission. Increasing highway competition threatened the viability of SP's local services and after the discontinuance of a pair of local trains in March 1959, the Budd RDC was transferred to the Northwestern Pacific. It was photographed at Ft. Seward, California, in May 1966. *Richard Jay Solomon*

NWP trainmen assist a passenger aboard Budd RDC No. 10 in May 1966. Traditionally, NWP long-distance trains terminated at Tiburon, California, where a ferry terminal provided a direct link to San Francisco. From the early 1940s, the terminus had been moved north to San Rafael, where passengers were offered a bus connection over the Golden Gate Bridge. In 1958, NWP services were cut back to just a Willits–Eureka operation that survived until the coming of Amtrak in 1971. *Richard Jay Solomon*

The Willits–Eureka Budd RDC operated on a twice-a-week schedule and provided passenger service to some very remote regions of California's Mendocino and Humboldt counties. The run along the Eel River Canyon geographically north of Dos Rios was especially scenic. *Richard Jay Solomon*

ECHO TUNNEL – NEAR McCRAYS
ON LINE OF NORTHWESTERN PACIFIC

Southern Pacific has the main north and south line along the Pacific Coast, serving the principle points of embarkation from San Diego to Portland. Naturally, troop trains must come first with us.

During World War II, SP was the third-largest passenger carrier and by far the largest in the West. Years of sagging passenger numbers were suddenly reversed. Whereas before the war SP advertisements encouraged people to ride its trains, during the war it cautioned civilian passengers against unnecessary travel. Even before D-Day, American railroads, including SP, were dreaming of ways to retain at least a portion of their newfound passenger business. Another centerpiece advertisement (in SP's November 14, 1943, public timetable) articulates SP's optimism for postwar rail travel.

Southern Pacific is host to thousands of men in uniform now "visiting" the West for the first time. Some had never been aboard a train until war came.

These sturdy youngsters with faces pressed against our train windows—will they want to travel in our western country again after the war? . . .

Among those who know these wartime tourists best are our "train riders"—the S.P. passenger representatives who act as liaison officers between the military and the railroad. The train riders tell us these boys are absorbed in what they see and surprised by the great distances.

"Gee, what a *big* country!" . . . "I think I'll come back some day and fish that stream!" . . . "What crops do they raise here?" . . . "Swell country, huh? I sure would like to look around out here again when this over!" . . . "My this is a pretty place"—and then with constant loyalty—"but you ought to see *my* home town!"

Yes, we think many of these service men now sampling the West will come back in peacetime. Then they'll see Yosemite and Lake Tahoe, Carlsbad Caverns, our giant Redwoods, Crater Lake, and other famous attractions. . . .

We look forward to the day when we can serve these men again, and in better fashion. After the war we will be able to provide service not only better than the wartime variety, but improved beyond previous peacetime standards.

The Northwestern Pacific (NWP) was formed in 1907 and jointly run by Santa Fe and Southern Pacific until 1929, when SP assumed full control of the lines. Until 1941, NWP operated intensive electric operations north of San Francisco. At one time, its lines provided a very good passenger service in Marin and Sonoma counties. This photo was made at the NWP's Echo Tunnel near McCrays, California. *Richard Jay Solomon collection*

Passenger figures had been rising before the war and this, combined with enormous wartime traffic, led SP management to believe that there was hope for passenger traffic after all. While SP was ineffective in competing head-to-head with the highway for intensive local traffic—their rural local passenger services had been on the verge of extinction before the war—Southern Pacific, like many American railroads, subscribed to the theory that their niche passenger market was in long-distance and luxury transport.

SP decided to install streamliners on all of its "four scenic routes" and followed up with enormous investment. This policy is where SP and like-minded carriers seem to have seriously miscalculated transport trends and the desires of the transport market.

The war greatly accelerated the development of automobile and, even more so, aircraft technology. This should not have caught the railroads entirely by surprise, since railroads had enjoyed improvements to diesel engine design as a result of wartime investment. SP and others did not appear to take heed. In addition to a massive surge in automobile ownership, after the war, cheap oil drove down gasoline prices, while state and federal aid for road-building was greatly increased. In the January 5, 1959,

Railway Age, a pro–passenger rail article titled "Political Realism and the Passenger Business" illustrated the inequities in public policy, highlighting expenditures between 1921 and 1956, during which $100 billion in public finds had created a vast highway network and the "rubber-tired" economy. As for air transport, Railway Age explained: "Domestic airlines received an estimated $440 million in nonpayback subsidy from 1939 through 1957" and "[The] government has spent more than $1.6 billion on airways since 1925—85 percent of it since 1945." The article further stated, "Government has invaded transportation on an increasing scale since 1945."

As they were structured, railroads provided neither convenience nor speed. Instead, railroads tried to put their best foot forward by offering luxury, comfort, and safety. Unfortunately, these criteria did not meet market demands, and after the war, the industry's market share declined rapidly. Southern Pacific, with its beautiful fleets of deluxe luxury streamliners, was caught short.

Other conditions hurt SP, too. The railroad's mountainous profile was not conducive to speed. In many cases, it simply took too long for SP's trains to travel over the road. Additionally, wartime equipment shortages had hampered SP's ability to get its streamliners up and running. By the time the streamliners were ready, the railroad had already lost its edge. In the case of the *Cascade* and *Sunset Limited*, the war had been over for five years by the time these trains were ready to roll.

Black Widow F units lead the *Shasta Daylight* at O'Brien in the summer of 1963. Large windows and deluxe accommodations had once made this train one of the best ways to travel between the Bay Area and Portland. On January 15, 1959, SP reduced frequency of this popular run to a triweekly operation and in 1966 it was canceled altogether. *Bob Morris*

If SP's rate of decline was typical, its deficits were exceptional. Ridership on most American railroads declined steadily after the tide of World War II traffic subsided. Except for a brief recovery during the Korean War, SP's traffic managers watched in horror and disgust as passenger numbers dropped each year despite the introduction of new diesels, faster schedules, and beautiful new trains. According to Garmany, in 1952 SP carried 4,541,000 long-distance passengers; just three years later the figure had declined by 25 percent to 3,332,000. As ridership dropped, so did passenger revenues—Garmany estimates that long-distance revenues declined 26 percent between 1951 and 1954.

The Russell Era

It became increasingly evident to SP management that it was losing the battle in competition for passenger traffic. By the mid-1950s, it seemed as if investment in streamliners had had little effect in curbing the decline in ridership. Under the leadership of Armand T. Mercier, SP had maintained a proactive, perhaps even romantic, outlook toward its passenger trains, authorizing expenditures for postwar streamliners and

The old SP Peninsula Line now has more passenger service than ever before. Today, service is provided by Cal-Train and operates on half-hourly intervals. In April 1992, a Cal-Train F40PH leads a San Jose–bound commute at South San Francisco. *Brian Solomon*

other improvements. Donald J. Russell, who had enjoyed a productive 31 years with SP before being appointed president, succeeded Mercier at the end of 1951. According to Don Hofsommer in *The Southern Pacific 1901–1985*, prior to Russell's appointment he had spent a decade working as an assistant to Mercier and "there was little doubt that he was headed for the corner suite in the executive department."

In the late 1940s, Russell had expressed reservations in regard to the future of long-distance passenger trains. He was well aware of the effects of auto and airline competition, and in his tenure as president he had a far more pragmatic outlook toward SP's passenger service than his predecessors. Under Russell, SP was transformed into a thoroughly modern freight railway.

Russell looked to rid SP of drains on its resources. Hofsommer explains that in 1953, SP finally shed its money-losing Pacific Electric (PE) city and suburban passenger

In February 1992, Cal-Train departs San Francisco for San Jose. The days of GS-4s on Commutes are long gone, but the passengers are still there. *Brian Solomon*

Southern Pacific's electric lines were hit hard by suburban development and increasing public automobile usage. Pacific Electric reached its zenith in 1926, when it operated 1,164 track miles in the Los Angeles basin. This was by far the largest electric interurban in the United States. Its trolleys were known as the "Big Red Cars"—this preserved example is operated at the Orange Empire museum at Perris, California. *Brian Solomon*

operations in the Los Angeles Basin, conveying most remaining lines (including bus services) to Metropolitan Coach Lines (MCL). He notes that PE's passenger miles had peaked in the 1920s and started running deficits as early as 1923. MCL intended to convert remaining railway operations to bus services as quickly as possible. Los Angeles, which had enjoyed the most extensive urban and suburban electric railway network in the United States, had also been a leader in highway-building, automobile ownership, and suburbanization.

Southern Pacific effectively ended its investment in new passenger equipment in 1954 when it ordered its dome cars for the *Daylight*s. One of its last major passenger investments was sharing construction costs of the New Orleans Union Passenger Terminal with six other railroads. One of the last new stations built in the United States, it was completed a generation after most other Union Station projects. Hofsommer notes that the railroads paid for this station out of profits.

Although SP initially continued to promote its passenger services under Russell, it hoped to curb deficits by implementing nominal cost-cutting. Among these measures was the introduction of its famous "Hamburger Grill Cars," which fulfilled dual goals of cutting food-service costs (dining cars had been losing money hand over fist for more than two decades) while simultaneously offering economy customers inexpensive and good food service.

In 1955 and 1956, SP exhibited the most dramatic shift in its passenger policies. Ridership continued to drop precipitously despite high-quality service—it seemed that no matter what the railroad tried, ridership continued to flee. Hofsommer notes that among Russell's

Southern Pacific dining cars operated at a loss. In 1954, SP introduced Hamburger Grill cars for coach passengers. This reduced operational costs while providing low-cost cafeteria-style food service to economy passengers. The cars were rebuilt at the Sacramento shops. In 1961, SP brought even greater austerity to railway dining with the debut of Automat Buffet Cars. *Southern Pacific photo, Bob Morris collection*

problems with passenger service was his assertion that the passenger business "consumed" too much of management's time. He wanted to focus on lucrative freight traffic and cut SP's passenger losses as quickly and as efficiently as possible.

Fred Matthews sums up the change in attitude under the Russell administration:

> We can see that the "Russellization" of the SP was the leading-edge case in the transformation of major railroads from a traditional to a late-twentieth-century enterprise. A. T. Mercier's SP was a multipurpose common carrier, accepting the obligation to offer broad public services by using cross-subsidization to maintain

In 1961, mail is transloaded to and from the *San Joaquin Daylight* at Fresno, California. Traditionally, many long-distance passenger trains carried U.S. mail as well as less-than-carload (LCL) express shipments that generated revenue and helped offset operating costs. In 1967, the U.S. Postal Service changed its distribution, ending most passenger train mail operations. As a direct result of this change, numerous trains were canceled on SP and on railroads all across the country. *Bob Morris*

what was needed but unprofitable. Russell's goal for the SP was a specialized freight carrier, using the latest technology to compete effectively for profitable traffic. Indeed, Russell's vision anticipated much of what happened [to the industry] after 1980, as Saunders describes in his essential book, *Main Lines*. Russell was so determined to transform the SP because he could see the changes occurring and coming—airplanes (he had been a pilot in World War I), trucks on freeways, universal auto use, perhaps (since he was a very impatient guy) the public impatience to reach destinations that would soon make a 16-hour coach train like the *Shasta Daylight* hard to sell.

Yet as Matthews relates in Chapter 1, it was not easy for SP to discontinue passenger services. The regulatory process slowed Russell's plans. In some cases it took years to convince governmental bodies to allow the removal of a train service. If Russell had had his way, undoubtedly many of SP's services would have been cut more quickly.

Initially, Southern Pacific targeted secondary trains that were the largest money losers. It also petitioned to reduce some still-popular trains to triweekly operation while combining other trains, operating two grades of service together on the same

Southern Pacific's passenger trains survived into the Interstate highway era. In this image, symbolic of the plight of the American passenger train, SDP45 3205 glides through Crockett, California, against the backdrop of highway bridges, including Interstate 80's crossing of the Carquinez Straits. How could railroads hope to compete with this massive public investment? *Bob Morris*

schedule rather than on separate trains. It also implemented other cost-cutting measures like the introduction of "Automat cars" with vending machines to replace costly dining cars. These efforts were met with protests from the public who believed SP was deliberately trying to discourage passengers. Regardless of its intent, SP's service cuts did nothing to encourage a ridership, which continued to plummet.

Among the first name trains cut was the poorly performing Houston–Dallas *Sunbeam* service, dumped on June 7, 1955. In July 1957, Coast Line overnight trains *Lark* and *Starlight* were combined as a single run. To passenger train enthusiasts this was a significant event because it ended the *Lark*'s status as a dedicated sleeping-car train. Another tradition died in 1958 when SP ended San Francisco–Oakland ferry services and closed the Oakland Mole railroad station and pier.

SP was an early proponent of curtailing daily services, even once-popular trains. At first, Russell wanted the *Shasta Daylight* reduced to a triweekly run during slack periods. After three years of wrangling, regulatory hurdles were cleared and beginning in 1959, the *Shasta Daylight*—once one of SP's star performers and one of its premier runs—only operated daily during peak-season traffic. A year later, the *Cascade* and *Sunset* also went to triweekly operation.

Cost-cutting also resulted in the simplification of paint liveries. In 1958, the variety of paint schemes then in vogue were effectively streamlined. The classy *Daylight* livery used on the PA/PBs and E units was replaced with the sharp, but more conservative, gray and scarlet scheme. The *Sunset Limited* livery became the standard scheme for most long-distance cars. No longer would trains carry distinctive equipment.

Despite draconian measures to lower SP's passenger deficit, in the 1960s, SP's accounting indicated it was still running the largest long-distance passenger deficit in the West. *The Future of Rail Passenger Traffic in the West*, the controversial study by Ely M. Brandes and Alan E. Lazar of the Stanford Research Institute, published in 1967, took a pessimistic viewpoint toward western rail service, essentially echoing SP's own business prerogatives. In 1950, SP's passenger deficits were $35.7 million, compared with Union Pacific's $30.2 million and Santa Fe's $20 million. By 1955, when railroads were hemorrhaging money, SP's deficit was $50.2 million, UP's was $46.2 million, and Santa Fe's was $40.9 million. In the 1960s, following the introduction of a more lenient discontinuance policy and subsequent cuts to their respective passenger networks, SP had a deficit of $36 million, UP was $34.8 million, and Santa Fe was $37.6 million. As Matthews describes, formulas for determining passenger-service profits and losses were greatly varied. How railroads weighed assets used by both freight and passenger services were open to interpretation.

In "Who Shot the Passenger Train?," David P. Morgan offered his perspective on the American rail passenger business: "But as secure in history as it is, the passenger train is dying today as a business. It loses money—lots of money." Later in the article he states:

> [T]he train is dying not because the jet is more efficient than the diesel, or because one out of every three Americans owns an automobile, or because railroad execs hate carrying people.
>
> Now, the agonizing fact is this: Few, astonishingly few, minds in or out of the industry comprehend the dilemma of the passenger train because of its complexity and its unorthodoxy. The problem has more facets than an armadillo has plates, and it may be irresolvable.

The whole passenger business, not just SP's, was in a downward spiral. It seemed that nowhere in the United States could railroads turn a profit running passengers. By the early 1960s, the federally funded interstate highway program was well underway and jet planes were common on domestic flights. In contrast, the quality and frequency of SP's trains had deteriorated to new lows. Its equipment was wearing out, its terminals were tired, and management was largely ambivalent to passengers. As the railroad downgraded its services, its passenger base evolved. SP had once aimed to provide a luxury service to appeal to high-class travelers, but cost-cutting and service reductions had made its trains less appealing. In the mid-1960s, its clientele was more economy-minded. Passengers boarding SP trains were no longer expecting to find deluxe accommodations. Railway enthusiasts decried this loss of status, but while the railroad was still required to run a service, it was not required to maintain luxury standards.

During the 1960s Donald Russell had his way; many of SP's best-known and historic train names vanished from the timetable. The *Overland* was unceremoniously combined with the *City of San Francisco* in 1962, and by the 1963 summer season it disappeared altogether. The *Shasta Daylight*, introduced with so much fanfare and advertising in 1949, made its final run on September 6, 1966.

Even more drastic measures were to come. In 1967, the U.S. Post Office implemented fundamental changes in mail distribution that effectively ended most Railway Post Office runs. This tipped the scales against remaining long-distance passenger trains that had relied on mail revenue to cover costs. SP President Benjamin F. Biaggini, appointed in 1964, announced, "the cold fact looms that the long-distance passenger train is dead and no amount of prayer or wishful thinking can bring it back to life."

In February 1968, the *Lark* rolled its last mile, and a few months later the *Golden State* was canceled.

Amtrak

During the late-1960s America's passenger train problem became a political issue. Growing highway congestion and increased airport traffic had made railway travel look appealing again. The Northeast had the greatest congestion and the most serious railroad crisis. The largest rail-passenger carrier, Penn Central, was embroiled in the world's largest financial debacle, effectively forcing federal government action to relieve American railroads from their intercity passenger burden. SP finally had the out it had been seeking. On the eve of the federally sponsored Amtrak, SP's final timetable included the daily *Coast Daylight*, *San Joaquin/Sacramento Daylight*, and San Francisco-to-Monterey *Del Monte* (the oldest name train operated by SP); the triweekly *Sunset Limited*, *Cascade*, and *City of San Francisco*; plus a triweekly Budd car (self-propelled rail diesel car) operation on its Northwestern Pacific subsidiary running from Willits to Eureka, California. At the end, SP's trains were very short, carrying just a fraction of the traffic it had moved two decades earlier.

Long-distance overnight trains such as the *Cascade* and the *Lark* were hit hard by the dramatic growth in airline travel after World War II. The *Cascade* was pictured here at Dunsmuir, California, in 1968. By this time the train was only operating triweekly.
Bob Morris

154

Amtrak's *Reno Fun Train* approaches Truckee, California, on April 26, 1975, hauled by six former SP F units. The paint had changed, but these locomotives were still doing what they were built for. *Brian Jennison*

On May 1, 1971, Amtrak assumed operation of most American intercity passenger trains. In the West, SP's intercity routes became an integral part of the Amtrak network. Initially, Southern Pacific continued to support its San Francisco–San Jose commutes. In 1980, these services were conveyed to a state agency (SP equipment and crews remained for a few more years). Southern Pacific has since faded from the scene—in 1997 it merged with Union Pacific and its mainlines are now freight corridors for that railroad.

Since the 1990s, California's mushrooming population and saturated highways have resulted in a renewed demand for regional passenger service, sparking a remarkable renaissance on former Southern Pacific passenger routes. A good example is the Capitol Corridor (San Jose–Oakland– Sacramento–Auburn), which now has a very good Amtrak service sponsored by the State of California. It was on the

central portion of this route that SP's consultants encouraged development back in 1933, to no avail.

The beautiful *Daylight*s and postwar streamliners are now just fond memory. Whereas SP's *Sunset Limited* was one of America's finest trains, the present-day *Sunset Limited* is one of Amtrak's worst-performing trains. Yet, Amtrak's *California Zephyr* and *Coast Starlight* are very popular with rail travelers and often sell out at peak times. Amtrak, however, remains underfunded.

Most travelers now endure the perils of pavement or the unpleasantness of airline travel; although Amtrak offers a rail option, it carries just a small fraction of intercity travelers. Nor does it have the flare or class of the old SP at its best.

The question remains: had SP made appropriate actions early enough could it have saved its passenger business? Should it have pursued subsidy in the 1920s and 1930s to allow its passenger services a fair shot at competing with public highways? To have taken such action, SP management would have had to overcome enormous internal hurdles, not to mention pursue politically unpopular public battles with the governments of the time. Given the prevailing business philosophy, the conservative attitude of its management, and public support for highway projects, such actions may have been impossible. We will never know.

A former SP Electro-Motive FP7 is lettered for new owner, Amtrak, on November 1, 1975. *Brian Jennison*

Bibliography

Books

Austin, Ed, and Tom Dill. *The Southern Pacific in Oregon.* Edmonds, Wash., 1987.

Beebe, Lucius. *The Central Pacific and the Southern Pacific Railroads.* Berkeley, Calif., 1963.

——————. *The Overland Limited.* Berkeley, Calif., 1963.

Best, Gerald M. *Snowplow: Clearing Mountain Rails.* Berkeley, Calif., 1966.

Borden, Stanley. *Northwestern Pacific Railroad.* San Mateo, Calif., 1949.

Bruce, Alfred W. *The Steam Locomotive in America.* New York, 1952.

Bush, Donald J. *The Streamlined Decade.* New York, 1975.

Cook, Richard J. *Super Power Steam Locomotives.* San Marino, Calif., 1966.

Daggett, Stuart. *History of the Southern Pacific.* New York, 1922.

Dorin, Patrick. *Amtrak—Trains & Travel.* Seattle, Wash., 1979.

Droege, John A. *Passenger Terminals and Trains.* New York, 1916.

Dubin, Arthur D. *More Classic Trains.* Milwaukee, Wis., 1974.

——————. *Some Classic Trains.* Milwaukee, Wis., 1964.

Dunscomb, Guy L. *A Century of Southern Pacific Steam Locomotives.* Modesto, Calif., 1963.

Farrington, S. Kip, Jr. *Railroads at War.* New York, 1944.

——————. *Railroading the Modern Way.* New York, 1951.

Frailey, Fred W. *Zephyrs, Chiefs & Other Orphans—The First Five Years of Amtrak.* Godfrey, Ill., 1977.

——————. *Twilight of the Great Trains.* Waukesha, Wis., 1998.

Garmany, John B. *Southern Pacific Dieselization.* Edmonds, Wash., 1985.

Hilton, George W. *American Narrow Gauge Railroads.* Stanford, Calif., 1990.

Hofsommer, Don L. *The Southern Pacific 1901–1985.* College Station, Tex., 1986.

Hollander, Stanley C. *Passenger Transportation.* Lansing, Mich. 1968.

Jennison, Brian, and Victor Neves. *Southern Pacific Oregon Division.* Mukilteo, Wash., 1997.

Kirkland, John F. *The Diesel Builders, Vols. I, II, and III.* Glendale, Calif., 1983.

Klein, Maury. *Union Pacific, Vols. I and II.* New York, 1989.

Lewis, Oscar. *The Big Four.* New York, 1938.

Marre, Louis A. *Diesel Locomotives: The First 50 Years.* Waukesha, Wis., 1995.

Pinkepank, Jerry A. *The Second Diesel Spotter's Guide.* Milwaukee, Wis., 1973.

Reed, S. G. *A History of the Texas Railroads.* Houston, 1941.

Ryan, Dennis, and Joseph Shine. *Southern Pacific Passenger Trains, Vols. 1 and 2.* La Mirada, Calif., 1986, 2000.

Saunders, Richard, Jr. *Main Lines: Rebirth of the North American Railroads, 1970–2002.* DeKalb, Ill., 2003.

——————. *Merging Lines: American Railroads, 1900–1970.* DeKalb, Ill., 2001.

——————. *The Railroad Mergers and the Coming of Conrail.* Westport, Conn., 1978.

Schafer, Mike. *All Aboard Amtrak.* Piscataway, N.J., 1991.

Signor, John R. *Beaumont Hill.* San Marino, Calif., 1990.

——————. *Donner Pass: Southern Pacific's Sierra Crossing.* San Marino, Calif., 1985.

——————. *Rails in the Shadow of Mt. Shasta.* San Diego, Calif., 1982.

——————. *Southern Pacific's Coast Line.* Wilton, Calif., 1994.

——————. *Tehachapi.* San Marino, Calif., 1983.

Shearer, Frederick E. *The Pacific Tourist.* New York, 1970.

Sinclair, Angus. *Development of the Locomotive Engine.* New York, 1907.

Solomon, Brian. *The American Diesel Locomotive.* Osceola, Wis., 2000.

——————. *The American Steam Locomotive.* Osceola, Wis., 1998.

——————. *Locomotive.* St. Paul, Minn., 2001.

——————. *Southern Pacific Railroad.* Osceola, Wis., 1999.

——————. *Super Steam Locomotives.* Osceola, Wis., 2000.

——————. *Trains of the Old West.* New York, 1998.

Stegmaier, Harry. *Southern Pacific Passenger Train Consists and Cars 1955–1958.* Lynchburg, Va., 2001.

Strapac, Joseph A. *Southern Pacific Motive Power Annual 1971.* Burlingame, Calif., 1971.

——————. *Southern Pacific Review 1952–1982.* Huntington Beach, Calif., 1983.

——————. *Southern Pacific Review 1953–1985.* Huntington Beach, Calif., 1986.

——————. *Southern Pacific Review 1981.* Huntington Beach, Calif., 1982.

Thompson, Gregory Lee. *The Passenger Train in the Motor Age: California's Rail and Bus Industries 1910–1941.* Columbus, Ohio, 1993.

Thoms, William E. *Reprieve for the Iron Horse: The Amtrak Experiment—Its Predecessors and Prospects.* Baton Rouge, La., 1973.

Wilson, Neill C., and Frank J. Taylor. *Southern Pacific: The Roaring Story of a Fighting Railroad.* New York, 1952.

Wright, Richard K. *America's Bicentennial Queen Engine 4449.* Oakhurst, Calif., 1975.

——————. *Southern Pacific Daylight.* Thousand Oaks, Calif., 1970.

Yenne, Bill. *History of the Southern Pacific.* Greenwich, Conn., 1985.

Periodicals

CTC Board—Railroads Illustrated. Ferndale, Wash.

Diesel Era. Halifax, Pa.

Diesel Railway Traction, supplement to *Railway Gazette* (UK). [merged into *Railway Gazette*]

Jane's World Railways. London.

Locomotive & Railway Preservation. Waukesha, Wis. [no longer published]

Official Guide to the Railways. New York.

Passenger Train Annual, Nos. 3 and 4. Park Forest, Ill. [no longer published]

Passenger Train Journal. Waukesha, Wis. [no longer published]

RailNews. Waukesha, Wis. [no longer published]

Railroad History. Boston, Mass. [formerly *Railway and Locomotive Historical Society Bulletin*]

Railway Age. Chicago and New York.

Railway Gazette, The. London.

Railway Mechanical Engineer. Unknown.

Railway Signaling and Communications. Chicago and New York. [formerly *The Railway Signal Engineer* née, *Railway Signaling*]

San Francisco Chronicle. San Francisco.

San Francisco Examiner. San Francisco.

Southern Pacific Bulletin. San Francisco.

TRAINS Magazine. Waukesha, Wis.

Today's Railways. Sheffield, UK.

Vintage Rails. Waukesha, Wis. [no longer published]

Timetables, Brochures, and Advertisements

Buell, D. C. The Railway Educational Bureau. Instruction Papers, Units CS.3 to CS.13; Railway Signaling. Omaha, Neb., 1949.

Northwestern Pacific Railroad Co. Timetable 22, 1943.

Southern Pacific Co. Coast Division Timetable 156, 1949.

——————. Public Timetables, 1930–1958.

——————. Western Division Timetable 243, 1947.

——————. "Your Daylight Trip," 1939.

——————. "Your Daylight Trip, Morning Daylight," 1949.

Southern Pacific Lines. Western Region Timetable 3, 1989.

Southern Pacific Lines, Texas & New Orleans Railroad Co. Time Table for San Antonio Division 178, 1943.

Southern Pacific Lines, Texas & New Orleans Railroad Co. Time Table for Victoria Division 68, 1944.